A Scotsman's Odyssey

A Scotsman's Odyssey

Published by The Conrad Press in the United Kingdom 2020

Tel: +44(0)1227 472 874
www.theconradpress.com
info@theconradpress.com

ISBN 978-1-913567-16-3

Typesetting and Cover Design by:
Charlotte Mouncey, www.bookstyle.co.uk

The Conrad Press logo was designed by Maria Priestley.

Printed and bound in Great Britain by Clays Ltd, Elcograf S.p.A.

A Scotsman's Odyssey

Ian G. Macpherson

To Gillian, Martin, and Keith

Contents

Chapter 1 – Dipping my toe in the water

I was introduced to water at an early age.

My father had been the Perth free-style swimming champion in the 1930s, and had me swimming before I went to school. I was a regular swimmer at Perth Baths, joined the Perth Amateur Swimming Club, got my swimming and lifesaving badges in the Boys' Brigade, and attained the Award of Merit of the Royal Lifesaving Association.

My interest in sailing was first aroused when I read Arthur Ransome's *Swallows and Amazons*, and the adventures of his young sailors in the Lake District had great appeal to me, but there was no tradition of sailing dinghies in Perth at that time. I had however spotted canoes on the River Tay from time to time, and when, aged sixteen I showed my father plans for building a canoe in the Boys' Own Paper, I was delighted when he suggested that we might build a canoe.

We sent off for the plans of a thirteen-foot Percy Blandford canoe, bought marine plywood for the frames, softwood lathes for the longitudinal stringers, and material for the skin from a canvas mill in Arbroath where my mother's uncle had been the works engineer. The canoe, which I named *Kelpie* had a red hull and a yellow deck. We launched her on the Tay at the Willowgate, a quiet channel behind a little wooded island beside the ancient Kinnoull Churchyard.

It surprised me to learn that the Tay was tidal up to Perth, twenty-three miles from the sea. The water did not actually turn salty as the tide rose at Perth, but it dammed up the fresh water, which rose several metres on spring tides. It reversed the flow under Perth Bridge and made it possible to paddle upstream to the North Inch, one of Perth's parks, a splendid venue for cricket, rugby and golf. At low tide there was a short rapid just below Perth Bridge and I delighted in running my canoe down the fast-moving water and darting to a sudden stop in the slack water just to one side of the main flow.

It wasn't long before I met members of the Tay Canoe Club on the river, and I soon joined the club which had a clubhouse and workshop just upstream of Perth Harbour. Its stalwarts who ran the club were Jack McLean and his whole family including wife Jean and even Grandfather McLean. The club organised canoe slalom competitions at Thistle Brig rapids below Stanley on the River Tay. Each weekend in the summer, club members camped at Fish Ponds, near Stormontfield, from where we could paddle up a mill lade to Thistle Brig. We slung ropes across the river from which we suspended the red and green poles, which marked the slalom gates.

I learned my river craft from the McLeans. 'Going downstream always go for the vee', they said, referring to the inverted v-shaped ripple pattern marking the river's deepest channel, which would be clear of most rocks. They showed me how to spot the most dangerous obstacles, rocks just below the surface of the river, invisible as the water rolled smoothly over them but indicated by the crescent of white broken water just beyond the rock. I learned how the slack water or backwater just beyond a visible rock was a place to slip into, to rest, using a 'Telemark Turn'. When leaving the backwater, you pointed the bow of the canoe into the stream but leant downstream so that the fast-flowing water caught the hull not the deck. If it hit the deck a capsize was a likely outcome.

In the 1950s canoe slalom was not the Olympic-recognised sport it is today. Fewer people owned cars and to travel to a canoe slalom competition most participants travelled by rail and carried a collapsible canoe in canvas valises.

The German *FolBot* was the classic collapsible canoe but, to my surprise, the Tay canoe club made their own collapsible slalom canoes. The canoe frame was in two flattened sections, which were opened up and inserted into the rubberised canvas skin, which Jack McLean made with his sewing machine. The frame was then stretched to fit snugly within the skin by a tensioning lever and the half-stringers joined by brass fittings at the centre of the boat. A floorboard, footrest and backrest were fitted and finally a central half-rib inserted into the cockpit was locked over the joined stringers and secured to the underside of the oval cockpit. The cockpit itself was a work of art, made of five ash laminations glued round a metal template, to provide two vertical slots. The inner one took the stiffened edge of the canoe skin and the outer slot took the stiffened edge of the canoeist's spray-sheet. Should the boat capsize the canoeist's weight pulled the edge of the spray sheet clear of the cockpit.

Under Jack's guidance I built my own collapsible canoe. It was silver-coloured, light, fast and highly manoeuvrable, a thoroughbred compared with my first rigid canoe, but needed some practice to keep on a straight course. None of our club slalom boats had a name. I tried it out on the rapids at Thistle Brig and was very pleased with its performance. I never won any slaloms but I was very impressed with the skills shown by our two best canoeists, Jack McLean and Dave Campbell, whom I did my best to emulate.

Once a year the club made a descent of the River Tay from Kenmore on Loch Tay to Perth over a summer holiday weekend. We camped overnight first at Kenmore and again at a little beach just upstream from Dunkeld House on the opposite bank. It was quite an adventure for a teenager, and I enjoyed these trips enormously. We paddled along beautiful stretches of river, with verdant wooded banks, saw herons, all sorts of ducks, and goosanders. We negotiated several rapids. We avoided the last waterfall at the Grandtully rapids, but shot the drop at Campsie Linn near Stanley. We also avoided the weir at Stanley. The most exciting stretches were on the rapids at Arkwright's Stanley Mills, which had names like 'Hellhole Corner.'

I had to give up the canoe club when I went to St. Andrews University in 1954 to take an honours degree in Physics, but I kept my two canoes.

Building my first canoe

Ian's slalom canoe *(Photograph by Star Photos)*

Chapter 2 – Royal Naval Volunteer Reserve

National Service was still in operation in 1954 and all young men were called up at the age of eighteen to serve in the forces for two years. Students had their call-up deferred till they graduated, but as I wished to serve in the Royal Navy, I was obliged to join the Royal Naval Volunteer Reserve in the university's naval unit. Its HQ was on HMS *Unicorn*, an ancient wooden frigate moored at Dundee. We were required to undertake a certain number of days training a year. These took place during university holidays.

I first went to sea as an ordinary seaman on 26 March 1955 on HMS *Chediston*, a wooden-hulled minesweeper, on a training voyage from Dundee to Oskarshamn, a little port on the Baltic coast of Sweden. Our captain was an RNVR lieutenant-commander. The petty officers were also RNVR. Only the ship's cook was a regular seaman.

As we left Scottish waters, we listened on the ship's radio to Cambridge winning the Boat Race. It was a very rough crossing in a strong northerly wind. The ship rolled as the cross-seas moved under her, and many of the crew, myself included, were seasick. It did not help when it started to snow. As we approached the Elbe Estuary in northern Germany, we were issued with heavy white polo necked sweaters and duffel coats. We entered the Kiel Canal, the shortcut to the Baltic Sea, and saw heavy ice encrusting the hulls of approaching cargo boats with timber deck cargoes. When we reached Kiel, the Baltic was covered with pack ice, which heaved slowly upwards and downwards as waves moved under it.

That night as I lay in my bunk, I could hear the ice floes scraping the hull a few inches from my head. A Swedish ice-breaker led us into Oskarshamn, on the Swedish coast opposite the northern end of the long island of Oland. The snow in port lay half a metre deep and it was very cold.

The next morning, we were given shore leave, but before dismissing us the chief petty officer issued each man with a condom. This caused great hilarity in some, but several students were shocked and refused to accept them. Compared with today's students many of us had led pretty sheltered lives; condoms were not easy to obtain and were not seen in shops or pharmacies.

We were the first RN vessel to visit the port since the war, and the town did its best to welcome us. They laid on a dance for us at the local community centre. The ship was open to the public during daytime and the captain invited local dignitaries to a cocktail party in the wardroom. We had wondered why Oskarshamn had been chosen for this courtesy visit to Sweden, and were now interested to learn that the captain's sister was married to a local businessman. She invited a group of us to visit her house where the captain's nephew hosted us in a wooden skittle alley in his parent's garden, stocked with a good supply of beer. A good time was had by all.

The voyage home was uneventful. We crossed the North Sea in brilliant sunshine. The wind was still from the north but by this time we had gained our sea legs. Taking my turn at the wheel during the hours of darkness it was difficult to counter the swing of the bows off course. The clicks of the gyroscopic compass dial as it turned were quite hypnotic and it was easy to lose concentration. Welcome cups of strong hot chocolate kept us alert. As we approached the Tay estuary in the early hours of the morning, we were cheered by the sight of the light of the Inchcape Rock Lighthouse and soon docked in Dundee.

I did my basic training for the RNVR in Portsmouth as one of a 'Schools and Universities' group. We were berthed on an old cruiser in Portsmouth harbour where we were taught the basics of seamanship and an introduction to navigation by a genial petty officer. When he took us to the naval gunnery school on Whale Island for a day's square-bashing, he transformed himself into a veritable martinet, shouting at us in true drill-sergeant style. Once we could handle rifles confidently on the parade ground, we were taken to a rifle range to learn how to fire them. It was in Portsmouth harbour that I had my first lesson in sailing on a naval whaler.

My third spell of training was with the regular navy, because I was unable to train with the university unit that year. I was posted to a battle class destroyer at Rosyth which was being taken out of mothballs and brought back to service readiness. Mess catering prevailed on this ship. Each mess of men decided on how and when their food would be served. The mess I was assigned to had opted for 'tea and tickler' for breakfast. As a tickler was a cigarette and I was a non-smoker I took a dim view of this and asked to be transferred to a mess providing a more substantial breakfast. I was relieved when my request was granted.

The work and tests to be done on the vessel were varied. First, she was attached to a very large buoy in the River Forth so that she could be swung around for the compasses to be adjusted.

When the tethering steel cables took the strain there was a bang as they parted, whipping back to the buoy on which sat the two ratings who had attached them to the buoy. Fortunately, neither was injured.

Next, the ship's motor launch was lowered on its davits to check their operation. A large number of ratings then lined up on deck to pull the vessel up again. As they pulled together there was another bang as a leading pulley block fixed to the deck gave way and struck an officer on the head, injuring him severely. He was rushed to hospital.

Now it was time to take the destroyer to sea for engine speed trials. We passed under the Forth Bridge, into the North Sea. It took several hours to work up to top speed. As quite a heavy sea was running, this was very uncomfortable and spray flew continuously over our bows. I was very seasick. Suddenly there was an explosion in the engine room. It took a long time to repair the damage and, to our dismay the speed trial would have to start all over again. This time there were no mishaps and we were glad to return to base at Rosyth.

One last incident ended our day. As we drew up alongside the dock, the ship did not quite come to a stop as it approached the end of the dock and the inevitable collision left the sharply angled destroyer's bow with a prominent large dent. I wondered how the captain would fare at his court martial!

After I graduated from St. Andrews University in 1958 with a B.Sc. Honours degree in Physics, I was interviewed in Chelmsford by Marconi and in Cheltenham by Smith's Aircraft Instruments. Both firms offered me a graduate apprenticeship but having had some teaching experience as a physics laboratory supervisor to medical students at St. Andrews, I decided to train in Edinburgh as a science teacher. Science teachers were in such short supply that Moray House College of Education cut the postgraduate training course to two terms instead of the usual three. I also enrolled in the Edinburgh University Diploma in Education course lasting three terms. Science teachers, still in very short supply, were then granted exemption from National Service, so I now resigned from the RNVR.

HMS *Chediston* at Oskarshamn

Shipmates on HMS *Chediston*, Ian is second from the right.

Chapter 3 – Career and family interlude

When I qualified as a teacher in April 1959, I got my first job in the Physics Department of George Heriot's School in Edinburgh. In July 1959 I married Gillian Brian who was an editorial assistant at Edinburgh University Press. We had first got together in the sixth year at Perth Academy, then both went to St. Andrews University where Gill took an M.A. in English and History, followed by a course at St. Godric's College, London. We bought a flat in Marchmont, Edinburgh, and my boating activities were abandoned for the moment as we concentrated all our efforts on setting up house together, and furthering our careers.

Gill became Departmental Secretary at the Mathematics Department of Edinburgh University. We had our first son Martin in February 1962, and in April 1962 we moved to Dornoch when I became Principal Teacher of Science at Dornoch Academy in Sutherland.

I did do some canoeing in the Loch Assynt area in Sutherland when I and Tom Strang, Principal Teacher of P.E. at the school, took a party of boys for an outdoor education trip involving orienteering, climbing, cave exploration at Inchnadamph, and canoeing on Loch Veyatie.

In 1964 I returned to Edinburgh to take up the new post of Principal Teacher of Physics at Liberton High School. We lived at Eskbank and in December 1965 our second son, Keith was born. I continued my interest in outdoor education and a group of us who taught at Liberton High School took teenage boys and girls on outdoor educational trips, this time based at Garth Youth Hostel in Glen Lyon in Perthshire. We canoed on the River Lyon.

In 1969 we moved to Paisley when I became the Schools Science Adviser for the County of Renfrew.

At Castle Semple Loch at Lochwinnoch a sailing club raced Mirror and GP14 dinghies. I had a few sailing lessons from one of the county's school sailing instructors, and proceeded to build a wooden Mirror dinghy from a kit.

It had a yellow hull and a white foredeck. I named it *Madrigal*. I then joined Castle Semple Sailing Club and raced my Mirror each weekend. I sold it eventually and bought a bigger glass fibre GP14 dinghy which I called *Blue Moon* and I raced at the loch regularly, till I cracked a rib in a capsizal in high winds.

I thought that maybe the time had come for me to move on to sail yachts, which are much more stable vessels.

Ian on his Mirror dinghy

Ian on his GP 14 *Blue Moon.*

Chapter 4 – The Firth of Clyde

The Firth of Clyde is an ideal cruising area for would-be yachtsmen. The upper firth is sheltered, with deep water, interesting sea lochs, and within easy reach of Glasgow. You don't have to own a yacht to have the opportunity to sail. Every boat owner needs a crew, and if he or she is a racing buff, a regular reliable crew is essential.

When my work colleague, Assistant Director of Education Duncan Graham asked me if I would like to crew for him one weekend in August 1977, I jumped at the chance. His boat *Charisma* was a twenty-seven-foot Contessa. The other crew member was also a colleague, David Lilley, Principal of the county's Outdoor Education Centre at Ardentinny on Loch Long a few miles to the north of Dunoon. We joined the boat at Inverkip Marina on Friday 12 August and sailed over to Port Bannatyne near Rothesay on the island of Bute, where we anchored overnight.

After an early breakfast on Saturday, we sailed to Rothesay for the start of the Clyde Cruising Club's annual Rothesay to Tarbert Race. A huge array of yachts manoeuvred at the starting line on a pleasant summer day with a moderate breeze to help us on our way. The starting gun sounded and we were off. The initial melee of boats gradually sorted itself out, the fleet rounded the southern end of Bute, and raced outside the island of Inchmarnock. Suddenly, about a hundred yards ahead of us a huge black and white killer whale leapt out of the water. I had never seen anything like it, and it made me first aware of how much wild life the yachtsman sees from time to time in Scottish waters.

We were not in the leaders of the fleet when the race ended at Tarbert on Loch Fyne but the race had been exciting and enjoyable. I was very taken with the picturesque little fishing port of Tarbert, where the many yachts were now tied up in 'trots', groups of boats tethered parallel to each other. I was told that etiquette demanded that, when going ashore crews from the outer boats in the trot should walk over the bows of each boat, preserving the privacy of the cockpit area.

We spent a noisy evening in a local pub and did not get much sleep when we returned to our boat as revelry continued on board many yachts into the small hours. The following day we returned to Inverkip via the beautiful Kyles of Bute. This was the voyage which got me hooked on sailing.

The following year on two cruises on *Charisma* we sailed to Lochranza at the north end of Arran and to Lamlash beside Holy Isle at the southern end of the island. I was getting to know the Firth of Clyde.

In 1979 I had more yacht racing on board *Sequoia*, a handsome thirty-five-foot wooden Nicholson Galion, belonging to Ian Colquhoun, whose son was a school friend of my son Martin; we competed in an overnight race round the Ailsa Craig, the steep-sided granite 'Paddy's Milestone' in the outer firth. I also sailed on *Sequoia* that year in the Round Bute Race and the Tarbert Race.

In 1980 I raced around the Clyde in Ron Spink's beautifully home-built yacht *Aerie Faerie*. I had met Ron through my work as Science Adviser. He was Master of Works in the Architect's

Department of the County of Renfrew Council. He oversaw the building of science laboratories, which I designed for new schools, and the architectural modifications I planned for existing school science departments.

Ron was a yacht-racing skipper par excellence. He had high standards of seamanship and demanded the same of his crews. A veritable martinet during a race, he was the perfect gentleman when socialising afterwards! I learned a great deal from him on the finer points of sail handling. He won many yachting trophies.

In 1973 I became Headmaster of Barrhead High School, and in 1976 I joined the Rotary Club of Barrhead. One of its members was Reay Mackay, who had a yacht chartering business, Gareloch Charters sailing out of Rhu Marina on the Gare Loch near Helensburgh. Reay suggested we take local teenagers for a weekend on a flotilla of his boats. Each boat would have an experienced skipper, a Rotarian to help, and a crew of young people. It sounded like an excellent local community project, so we went ahead with his idea, and enlisted the help of Barrhead High School and St. Luke's High School to select young people who would benefit from this experience.

Our first such weekend was on 19 April 1980 from Troon Marina. I skippered *Sea Eagle* a twenty-eight-foot Seal, with my son Martin to help, and five Barrhead boys on board. We sailed over to Lamlash on Arran in a rising wind which scattered the little fleet and we had to reef down quickly as the wind rose to gale force. We dropped the anchor at Lamlash, sheltered by the Holy Isle. It was a rough introduction to sailing for our inexperienced crew, but we had a quieter return the next day to Troon and the boys had an experience they would never forget.

Sailing on *Aerie Faerie*, Ron Spinks and Ian

Ian and crew on first sailing weekend

Chapter 5 – RYA Yachtmaster Offshore

By this time, I had plans to charter yachts for more extended cruising and realised that I needed to get some formal qualifications in sailing. I spent three winters at navigational and seamanship courses at Glasgow Nautical College working towards RYA Yachtmaster qualifications. As well as gaining these shore-based course certificates, I needed to take a practical yachtmaster's course which I did from 8-14 August 1981 on *Northern Spray*, a ten-metre Moody from the Scottish National Watersports Training Centre on the Isle of Cumbrae.

RYA Yachtmaster regulations also obliged me to log fifty days living on board a cruising yacht in commission, 2,500 nautical miles logged at sea, in tidal waters, including at least five passages of over sixty nautical miles, on at least two of these acting as skipper, and including two which had involved overnight passages.

Over the next few years, I chartered yachts to cruise around the West Coast of Scotland to build up my sea miles and hours. One of the skippers who had sailed alongside me on one of the other yachts at the Young Peoples' Sailing Weekends was a voluntary Ocean Youth Club mate. I was impressed with his skill in getting his young crew to steer, navigate and handle the boat in a very short time. He said he did as he usually did on the OYC Scottish Area yacht, *Taikoo*, a seventy-two-foot John Clark designed ketch with a complement of eighteen.

The OYC, he said, was always looking for voluntary mates to sail with their full-time professional skippers. I decided to apply to the OYC as a trainee voluntary mate. I enjoyed sailing with teenagers, and a larger yacht would make more extended passages, which would let me build up my sea miles more quickly.

I was accepted by the OYC and my first voyage as a trainee mate on *Taikoo* was from 14-19 April 1982 out of Inverkip Marina to Lamlash, Lochranza and back through the Kyles of Bute.

Everything on *Taikoo* was on a much larger scale than on yachts I had sailed on previously. There was only one winch on board, a huge one in the centre of the cockpit, which handled sheets from the mainsail. All other ropes were handled by blocks and tackles. Raising the mainsail and lifting the anchor via its capstan required several hands, deliberately so, to develop teamwork.

On 22 March 1982 I was ready to take my oral examination for RYA Coastal Skipper, at the Royal Northern Yacht Club at Rhu. My RYA examiner was Ron Hockey, who grilled me on my sailing experience and tested my Morse code. He passed me and, in more relaxed conversation afterwards, I realised that he had interviewed me many years before at Smiths Aircraft Instruments, Cheltenham, when I had been interviewed for a graduate apprenticeship. I also learned that he was the current Scottish Area Governor of the Ocean Youth Club.

I got to know him better on OYC mates training cruises, but it was many years later in a BBC TV documentary that I learned of his distinguished war flying career in the RAF and SOE. In a light aircraft, he had flown the Czech assassins into Czechoslovakia who killed the notorious Nazi Reinhard Heydrich.

I qualified as an OYC first mate in October 1982, but mates training was continuous. Safety at sea was taken very seriously. The OYC ran intensive training cruises for mates on *Taikoo*, as handling a large yacht was a quite different sailing experience for most of us. Handling heavy sails required teamwork. We practised man overboard drills over and over again, each taking his or her turn at the wheel, getting used to manoeuvring the large seventy-two-foot vessel under sail and under engine.

We became confident in dead reckoning our course, and confirming it by fixing our position, which we marked on the chart every hour, using hand-bearing compasses and prominent landmarks to triangulate our position. We were encouraged to use transits, lining up two known landmarks, which gave a definite line of position on the chart whenever the two marks were in line.

One of our first mates, Malcolm McArthur, had a Rival 34, *Rona of Melfort*, which was used for preparing us for the RYA Yachtmaster Offshore practical examination. I finally qualified as an RYA Offshore Yachtmaster on 11 October 1987 after a two-day assessment at sea on *Rona*.

I sailed with the Ocean Youth Club as a mate for twenty-one years. Its aim was to give boys and girls between the ages of fourteen and twenty-five an enjoyable and adventurous experience at sea, involving mixing with others from varied backgrounds, teamwork, initiative, responsibility, and the wide range of activities associated with sailing a yacht safely. This included working with others in a watch day and night under the supervision of a mate. They also did their share of cleaning and cooking.

Discipline was quickly accepted. It was obviously essential for sailing safely. Responsibility was real. On a night passage the lives of all sleeping below, were in the hands of the watch on duty. Girls and boys on board were in roughly equal numbers, as were male and female mates.

Some trainees paid their own way; others were sponsored by schools, social work departments, charities, and Rotary Clubs. Life on board could be quite a shock for some of the youngsters from deprived backgrounds who had grown up in a very limited environment. I remember one boy who dived into the Firth of Clyde soon after joining the boat. As his head emerged from the water he spluttered,

'Bloody hell, naebody telt me the watter wis salt!'

Another boy arrived with a bag of tinned food, refusing to eat anything else! Home cooking on board was an eye-opener for him. He had not realised that we would be teaching him some basic cooking skills. On another occasion, moored overnight in Rothesay on *Taikoo*, I was in the galley preparing chilli con carne for the evening meal when a group of youngsters saw me put red raw mince into a large hot casserole.

'We're no' eatin' that!' exclaimed one lad, but that evening he and his pals scoffed the lot!

It was not long before I persuaded the Rotary Club of Barrhead to sponsor local teenagers from Barrhead. We sent them on voyages on *Taikoo* to Tarbert on Loch Fyne, to St. Kilda, and to Barra.

At that time the Ocean Youth Club, which was a sail training charity, had its headquarters in Gosport, and the UK was divided into six OYC Areas, each with its own large yacht. Area Governors were elected by local voluntary mates, and served as company directors on the OYC Board for three years. The yachts had full-time professional skippers assisted by voluntary bosuns, who were recruited from keen youngsters who had sailed with the OYC previously. In time, some of these became OYC voluntary mates. As mates we could opt to sail on cruises on any of these yachts, which gave us the opportunity to widen our experience with different skippers.

Ian helming *Taikoo*

OYC ketch *Taikoo*

Chapter 6 – Yachting Rotarians

Our sailing weekends for Barrhead teenagers had been so successful that I now organised sailing weekends for my fellow Rotarians, on Reay Mackay's charter boats.

The first of these on 15 May 1982 was to Tarbert on Loch Fyne from Rhu Marina, on Gareloch Charters yacht *Asterix*, a thirty-foot Dufour. We returned by the Kyles of Bute with ideal sailing conditions for the whole weekend. In contrast, our next trip on *Columba of Iona*, a Moody 33, in September 1982 was a much more demanding trip. Gale force wind on the return voyage from the Kyles of Bute obliged us to raise the storm jib with double-reefed mainsail.

Hearing of our sailing trips, two other Rotary Clubs, Paisley Callants and Kirkintilloch, challenged us to a race from Inverkip to Rothesay in May 1983.

It was a light-hearted affair and when the little fleet was becalmed, we noticed through binoculars that the Paisley Callants boat was sailing backwards with their sails up. When challenged they denied having used their engine!

The next year when we organised the race, we drew up proper sailing rules to bring some order into the event, and the Barrhead branch of the Bank of Scotland gave us a brass bell as a race trophy, which we called The Barrhead Bell.

In the following years more boats took part over a weekend. On the Saturday we raced round the buoys in the Firth of Clyde between Largs and Gourock with the finishing line at

Rothesay. We ended the day with a barbecue at an anchorage at the Kyles of Bute, and we had a leisurely sail home on the Sunday. It became an annual event for the Clyde fleet of the International Yachting Federation of Rotarians, which provided officials to run the event.

In May 1984 I skippered the Barrhead boat *Arabesque*, a Sigma 33, which won the Barrhead Bell trophy for the club for the first time. We won it again in May 1994, and May 1995 on *Southern Comfort*, a Moody 31 owned by my friend Gerry Fretz. In May 2000 we won the trophy on my own boat *Rum Runner*, a Nicholson 35. In 2013 and 2014 we won the trophy two years running in Reay Mackay's Moody 33, *Kiri*. These were the last two races for the Barrhead Bell trophy.

I had now introduced several Rotary friends to sailing, and had no difficulty in persuading some of them to sail further afield with me. In September 1983 we chartered *Contessa of Lorne*, a Contessa 32, from Ardtalla Yacht Charters at Oban for the weekend. We sailed up Loch Linnhe towards Fort William in a rising south-westerly wind with minimum sail. When the wind reached gale force, we dropped the sails, and motored under the road bridge into Loch Leven.

We sought shelter at Bishop's Bay, a secluded anchorage just beyond the bridge. There were six of us on board and after supper we played cards while the wind roared and the rain came down in sheets. It was going to be a demanding voyage back to Oban against this wind in the morning.

Putting a good face on it, we set off, but the wind was still very strong from dead ahead and a heavy sea buffeted us. After an hour of tacking we had made little headway, even with assistance from the engine, and the Island of Shuna was still some way off. We prudently ran back to Bishop's Bay and tethered the boat to a substantial buoy in the middle of the bay. We would have to leave the boat here till the high wind abated. Two of the crew went back to Oban by bus and brought our cars back to Bishop's Bay. I phoned Ardatalla yachts to say we would have to return the boat a day or two late. Before leaving, I put out our anchor over the stern to stop the boat swinging too much. The following Wednesday three of us returned, and sailed the boat back to Oban by the Sound of Shuna and the Lynn of Lorne in Force 6-7 wind and rainy squalls.

Two years later we had a more successful trip from Oban to Barra in the Outer Hebrides. We chartered *Canta Libre*, a Rival 34 from Ardatalla Yachts. I was skipper, Arthur Cooper was mate, and the crew were Owen Evans, Mike Pegg, Ron McKechnie and my son Martin. This was my first voyage over sixty nautical miles which I logged for my yachtmaster's assessment.

Our first stop was at Loch Aline on the Sound of Mull which I had visited previously on an OYC trip. Fine sand has been quarried here for many years in the only underground sand mine in the UK. The sand is used for making optical glass. The next day we had a pleasant sail past the Point of Ardnamurchan and Coll, to Barra, in bright sunshine. We had light winds off Barra, so put mackerel lines over the stern and caught half a dozen mackerel for our supper.

We anchored at Castlebay, Barra beside Kisimul Castle, and I reported the safe arrival of *Canta Libre* by VHF radio to Clyde Coastguard. They asked if Ian Macpherson was on board. When I answered yes, they suggested that on future trips we should let our wives know the name of our yacht! Mike's wife had been alarmed to hear on the radio news that a yacht had been in difficulties in the Outer Hebrides and thought that it might have been us, so had phoned the coastguard for more information.

The next day we crossed over to Canna, anchoring bedside the church on Sanday, at Canna harbour. We progressed to Arinagour on Coll, then past Dutchman's Cap in the Treshnish Isles and Fingal's Cave on Staffa to Bunessan on Mull. As the sun set, we feasted on fresh prawns bought from a passing fishing boat.

Our last stop before Oban was the beautiful anchorage of Puldoran, on the Isle of Seil. On a warm sunny evening we walked over the hill to the pub at Seil Sound, beside the 'Bridge over the Atlantic.' Having circumnavigated Mull, where could we go next? It was time to explore Skye.

Winning the Barrhead Bell
Left to right, Mike Pegg, Neil Dryburgh, Ian,
John Ewing and John Gray

Chapter 7 – Skye

Our first trip to Skye was on Saturday 26 July 1986. Leaving our cars at Mallaig, we took the ferry across the Sound of Sleat to Ardvasar, where we collected *Goodbye Girl*, a Rival 34 from our charterer Sleat Marine Services. There were five of us on this voyage, myself as skipper, Arthur Cooper as mate, Owen Evans, Mike Peg, and my son Martin.

On Sunday we sailed north-east up the Sound of Sleat, through the narrows at Kylerea into Loch Alsh, then eastwards into Loch Duich. We dropped the anchor at Ob Totaig opposite Eilean Donan Castle. Before supper, Martin and I rowed ashore in the dinghy and climbed up to the ancient ruined broch that overlooked the anchorage.

The next day we continued though the Kyle of Lochalsh past Scalpay and Raasay to Portree, where we anchored overnight. There were high winds on Tuesday and we found shelter in the lovely landlocked harbour of Acairseid Mhor on the Island of Rona. Our next leg took us to Shieldaig on Loch Torridon. Our last port of call was the picturesque village of Plockton on Loch Carron. We returned the yacht to Ardvasar, before taking the ferry back to Mallaig.

In 1987 I decided to make a sixty nautical miles non-stop voyage which was one of the requirements for yachtmaster assessment. We would collect the boat from Ardvasar on Skye, take the yacht over to Inverie Bay on Loch Nevis, and make that our starting point for a non-stop voyage southward to Colonsay.

My crew this time was Arthur Cooper as mate, Tim West, Owen Evans, John Ewing, and Dan Malloy. The boat was *Gwenny's Rival*, another Rival 34 from Sleat Marine Services.

We collected the yacht from Ardvasar on 8 August, taking the boat to Glascoile on Inverie Bay that afternoon, where we anchored, marking the anchor position with a white fender tied to a light line as an anchor buoy. The crew took the outboard dinghy to the pub at Inverie that evening, while I got out the charts to plan tomorrow's voyage. Our course would take us south to Mull and Iona, through the shallow Sound of Iona and the Torran Rocks, and on to Colonsay. It would require an early start at first light.

After a hearty breakfast, we started the engine and got ready to raise the anchor in semi-darkness. I took the wheel and Arthur operated the electric anchor winch. As we crept forward towards the anchor at low revs, I suddenly saw the white anchor buoy approaching the boat at speed. It was obvious that its line had fouled the propeller shaft! I killed the engine and shouted to Arthur to stop raising the anchor. Someone would have to dive under the boat to free the fouled anchor buoy line. It would have to be me. I changed into my bathing trunks, put on a face mask, and with a safety line tied round my waist I slipped into the water from our rubber dinghy tied to the stern. I gasped as the cold water hit me, and pulled myself quickly back on to the dinghy to recover. After splashing more water on to myself to acclimatise to its temperature, I dived under the yacht and with difficulty in the dim light, freed three turns of the anchor line from the propeller shaft. I was glad to get back on board, dried myself off, and got into warm clothing as quickly as I could.

We now set off, a beautiful sunny day developed, and fair winds sped us southward. We passed Eigg, Muck and Coll and close to Dutchman's Cap in the Treshnish Isles. We a had a good view of Fingal's Cave as we passed Staffa. As we approached the Sound of Iona I checked the tides to ensure that we had enough water under us in the sound. Very quickly we were amid the Torran Rocks where careful navigation was required, and as the sun was close to setting we arrived at Colonsay and anchored off Scalasaig.

When we went to the inn at Scalasaig after supper, we found that it had been Regatta Day and everyone was now off to a barbecue on the golf course. We were swept into cars and taken to a bonfire where everyone on Colonsay seemed to be making merry. The hamburgers were consumed and the whisky flowed.

It was getting very late and we had had a long day so we all returned to the boat except Dan who decided to stay a little longer. We discovered next morning that when he was ready to leave, a kind man had given him his car keys, saying he could leave the car at the inn. Unfortunately, Dan had to park the car before he reached the inn as the gear handle came away in his hand!

We now sailed north towards Skye, and anchored overnight at Puldoran, the sheltered anchorage at the north end of the Isle of Seil. The next day we made a short stop at Oban to pick up provisions, then sailed up the Sound of Mull to Tobermory. Arisaig was our next port of call with an interesting winding approach channel through the rocks to negotiate.

Arisaig was ideally placed for a short passage out to Rum the following day. We anchored in Loch Scresort, and visited Kinloch Castle built by the eccentric Edwardian business magnate George Bullough. We perused his game books listing the many birds shot on Rum by his guests, and listened to operatic music on his mechanical orchestrion which entertained his dinner guests with organ music, trumpets and drums. The orchestrion is similar to a fairground organ, the notes of each musical work being controlled by a continuous sheet of coded perforated paper.

We now returned to Ardvasar. It had been a memorable cruise. Where next? The Outer Hebrides.

Gwenny's Rival at Colonsay

Ian and Dan Malloy on *Gwenny's Rival* at Colonsay

Chapter 8 – Suspicious activity on Harris

Little had we known that this trip would be so eventful. It was Sunday 7 August 1988 and we had awoken to a quiet day on Skye. We had left Loch Scavaig under the Cuillins at 0930, bound for Tarbert in Harris in calm weather, but as we reached Soay the wind suddenly increased from the southeast. As we approached Dunvegan Head the wind freshened and wave crests began to break. At 1200 the shipping forecast announced a gale warning 'soon' in sea area Hebrides, so we made for Loch Dunvegan and anchored near Dunvegan Castle in a sheltered spot on the Dunvegan Head shore. It was a 'stourie' night with strong winds and heavy rain. We relaxed with card games of 'Black Bess'.

Our sailing yacht, *Mallish*, a Rival 38 on charter from Ardtalla Yachts of Ardvasar on Skye, was a solid thirty-eight-foot ocean-going vessel, and carried a crew of six. There was myself as skipper, Arthur as mate, John, Charlie, Tim and Owen.

The weather was fine and hazy the next morning. We left Dunvegan at mid-day with a steady moderate wind from the south-west, and reached East Loch Tarbert on Harris at 1630. We took on water at the pier, and on the recommendation of the harbour master we anchored in five metres clear of the MacBraynes ro-ro ferry terminal.

While the crew went ashore to buy food, I stayed on board to plan our next itinerary. I was alerted by a call from the skipper of a Norwegian yacht which had come alongside. He asked the way to Scalpay where he wanted to tie up at a pier as he did not have a good anchor. I rowed over to show him the Clyde Cruising Club Sailing Directions, which I passed up to him in a plastic wallet.

I climbed aboard and copied a sketch of Scalpay north harbour for him from the sailing directions. I returned to our boat and he sailed off for Scalpay without having anchored.

In the late afternoon, a distinctive dark red car stopped on the pier and a man wearing a fawn raincoat and soft hat got out. He looked over in our direction. Could he be a policeman, and why was he so interested in us? We laughed at our suspicions as we went ashore that evening to the Harris Hotel, where we had baths and a drink or two.

The weather forecast was not good for the next day. Heavy rain and gale force winds were expected, so we planned a day ashore to explore the southern end of Harris. For this we needed transport, and Arthur had a chat with the usual fount of all local knowledge, the village post-mistress, who put us in touch with the local garage owner who had a minibus for hire. Unfortunately, its battery was flat but with six able-bodied sailors on hand we were able to get it going with a push start.

We drove down the western side of Harris whose Atlantic beaches were attractive but empty of people on this wet blustery day. I was keen to visit the medieval church of St. Clements at Rodel, built around 1500 A.D. It contained the elaborate tomb of its builder, clan chief Alexander MacLeod of Dunvegan and Harris. One of its carvings shows a birlinn, the traditional square-rigged galley of the Hebrides. It was portrayed on the cover of the Clyde Cruising Club Sailing Directions for the Hebrides. I had noted how the ropes supporting the mast were attached to it in exactly the same way as the mast of the little Mirror dinghy in which I had learned to sail. The ancient church was busy, with lots of foreign tourists, - a fascinating place.

We had lunch at the hotel pub at Rodel. The hotel, which had hosted the Queen on a visit to Harris in 1958 was now closed and derelict, but the pub was still in use and well supported by locals. We noticed a pipe-smoking man in a corner whom we joked looked more like a policeman than a local.

We returned to Tarbert via the rocky east coast road, stopping at a fish farm to order a whole salmon for our evening meal. It would be delivered to the boat later.

Just after we returned to the boat, we noticed the reappearance of the red car and its mysterious driver. The salmon duly arrived, neatly packaged up, and after an enjoyable supper we got ready to go ashore for the evening.

As we got on deck to get the dinghy ready, the red car made its third appearance. Two men got out and the one in the fawn raincoat called out:

'We want to speak to you!'

Arthur and I went ashore in the outboard dinghy and hovered just off the pier.

'Who are you?' I asked.

'Police officers!' was the reply.

I asked for identification and the warrant card of a detective inspector was produced. They explained that they suspected that drugs would be landed from a yacht in the Hebrides that weekend. All yachts were being searched and would we mind if they had look round our yacht. As we had nothing to hide, I agreed.

A uniformed policeman now appeared and I took the three policemen out to the yacht. The uniformed policeman told me that I had been seen passing a plastic-covered package to the Norwegian yacht yesterday which had moved off without anchoring. I could see how that could have seemed suspicious and explained that the Norwegian had only been asking me for directions. Now I wondered what the police thought had been in the package delivered to the boat before supper-time, and I hoped that any previous clients who had chartered the yacht had left nothing untoward in the vessel.

The detective inspector asked for our names, dates of birth, addresses and occupations. I was a headmaster, Arthur had a builder's business, John was a former Rolls Royce engineer who had an industrial abrasives business, Charlie was a senior Rolls Royce engineer, Tim was a university engineering lecturer and Owen was a chartered accountant. I produced charter documentation from Ardtalla Yachts.

'Hmm… It's a very well-equipped yacht,' said the detective inspector as he looked around. They proceeded to rummage the vessel.

Charlie was quite amused.

'If I were looking for drugs,' he said, 'I would look in the head' (the boat's WC).

Stony-faced, the policemen continued their search, finding nothing.

'Where are you going over the next few days?' asked the detective inspector.

'We leave early tomorrow morning to catch the favourable tide for Portree,' I replied, 'then on to Ardvasar via the Kyle of Lochalsh to return the yacht.'

The passage to Portree was uneventful, but at a dockside pub at Portree that evening, Arthur spotted the same pipe-smoking gentleman who had lunched alongside us at Rodel.

'It's too much of a coincidence,' said Arthur, 'I am going to have it out with him!'

He turned to confront him, but the man had vanished. Arthur went out to the door of the pub and saw him join an unmarked blue launch, which disappeared into the darkness.

The next morning, a possible reason for police surveillance at Portree that evening suggested itself. IRA bombings had been particularly prevalent in 1988, and as we sailed down the Sound of Raasay towards the Kyle of Lochalsh, we passed two ships at anchor, the RN frigate HMS *Battleaxe*, and the Royal Yacht *Britannia*.

When we sailed past Kyle of Lochalsh at mid-afternoon the tide was against us. Barely making headway, we spotted an otter amongst the seals on the rocks east of the village. With a moderate north wind behind us, I started to motor-sail against the tide with main and genoa. Three Wayfarer dinghies suddenly shot past us with the tide behind them.

'Do you know the tide is against you?' the last helmsman shouted.

'We sure do!' was my reply.

As we approached the narrows at Kyle Rea our speed log read seven and a half knots but the pylons ahead were no closer. I increased engine revs and crept a little closer to the Skye shore, which let us gain on the tide.

When we reached Glenelg the ferry swung out from the Skye side then turned with the tide and passed safely under our stern. The yacht swung about in the strong eddies, but flipping the genoa over to sail goose-winged gave us another half knot as we reached the calmer waters where the Kyle widens considerably at Glenelg village. It had taken us an hour and twenty minutes to sail two miles.

Once past Glenelg we were suddenly becalmed so dropped the sails and continued under engine, but ten minutes later it returned with a blast from the west. With main up alone, we were making six knots in seconds, and shot past Gavin Maxwell's house, Camas Fearna, of *Ring of Bright Water* fame. The wind dropped off Isle Oronsay and from there we motored to Ardvasar. It had certainly been a cruise to remember.

Ian navigating

Tarbert, Harris

Chapter 9 – The Northwest Highlands

When I was a teenager we spent a family camping holiday in the north-west of Scotland, but it was not till July 1992 that I was able to explore its rugged coast from the sea. I organised a cruise to the Northwest Highlands with six of my fellow OYC voluntary mates, all keen to increase their logged sea miles for an RYA Yachtmaster qualification.

We chartered a forty-one-foot Sigma yacht from West Highland Charter, based at Badachro, an attractive village on Loch Gairloch in Wester Ross. I was skipper, and I had three RYA Coastal Skippers as mates. They were my friend Arthur again as first mate, Ken and Alex as second mates. The other crew members were trainee mates, and all women – Cath (Alex's wife), Lorna and Betty. Betty was a go-ahead old age pensioner who golfed, skied and abseiled.

The charter company manager was an hour late in meeting us on the pier. He explained that the previous chartering group had lost the boat's rubber dinghy, which he had been unable to recover. We would have to take his spare rubber dinghy. This was to cause us a few problems as this dinghy leaked and we had to put wine corks into its leaking valves to stop its deflating. This could not be done till we had drunk a few bottles of wine.

We arrived on 4 July laden with food for seven, for seven days. The food was ferried out to our yacht, which was called *Birlinn of Chlann Ranald*.

We were surprised to find a real birlinn tied up at Badachro.

This replica highland galley had been rowed to the Faroes after calling into the Shetland Islands for a rudder repair. It made it to the Faroes, but the seas were so stormy there that rather than risk a dangerous landing, the Faroese Coastguard took the boat in tow and brought it all the way back to Scotland. It had arrived at Badachro the day before we arrived.

To familiarise ourselves with the yacht, we had a pleasant evening sail to the island of Longa in Loch Gairloch and returned to Badachro to spend an hour or so in the pub, where one of the birlinn's rowers played us a pibroch on his bagpipes at sunset. We spent our first night on the boat on our mooring at Badachro.

Next morning, we set sail in light winds to Staffin Bay on Skye but as the wind was blowing into the anchorage, we sailed on to Acairseid Mhor, the very sheltered large anchorage on Rona, which I had visited in 1986. We had it to ourselves till a group of young people from the outdoor centre on Raasay appeared out of the blue, and were picked up by a speedboat from Raasay.

On Monday morning we sailed north to Lochinver, but had to motor in light winds from Priest Island onwards. On the way we met a school of about twenty black and white dolphins. For ten minutes they played around the yacht crossing and criss-crossing the bows and showing their blow holes as they surfaced.

A new harbour was under construction at Lochinver. We picked up a mooring buoy near an RNLI lifeboat moored next to the pier. It was not till next morning that I discovered that our mooring buoy was in fact a marker attached to the anchor securing the lifeboat's mooring. Luckily it had been a quiet night and we had not dragged out the lifeboat's mooring. We had a run ashore for showers at the Fishermen's Mission which was used as a community centre.

Tuesday morning began with a heavy fog which delayed our departure till noon. There was no wind so we motored in drizzle to the island of Handa, a bird sanctuary at the northern end of Eddrachillis Bay. We passed The Old Man of Stoer, a huge rock stack near the Point of Stoer.

Handa was inhabited until about 1850 and the oldest widow there was recognised as their queen. Poor harvests led to its evacuation and there are only a few ruins and tombstones left now. Burials were common on Handa at a time when wolves on the mainland tended to dig up graves.

Tidal streams run strongly in the Sound of Handa, so we went ashore in two groups as we did not want to leave the anchored boat unattended. I led the first group and as we landed on a beautiful sandy beach an attractive young woman suddenly appeared from nowhere. It was as if she had emerged from the rocks!

She introduced herself as the warden for the island, which is managed by the Scottish Wildlife Trust. She asked us to put a pound each in an honesty box in a nearby display shelter, which contained information boards about the birds, and she asked us to keep to the paths as we crossed the island to the cliffs and stacks where the birds congregated.

We walked two miles across the island to the Great Stack, a rock formation covered with guillemots, razorbills, kittiwakes and puffins. On the way, we saw oystercatchers, grouse, great skuas or bonxies, and long-tailed skuas.

On the way back there was a 'whoosh!' around my ears and

I realised I was being attacked by a bonxie whose nest must have been nearby. I didn't linger. Skuas are pirate birds who force other seabirds to give up their catch in mid-air. They then catch the released fish.

After a meal, we motored through a maze of islands to anchor at Badcall Bay, completely sheltered from the Atlantic.

The next morning the wind rose, and we had a fast passage round the Point of Stoer. As we passed the Old Man of Stoer, we watched a climbing party tackling the stack. One swam across the short gap to secure a rope, then the others made a Tyrolean traverse across.

The sun came out and we had a splendid sail in moderate wind to the Summer Isles near Achiltibuie at the entrance to Loch Broom. We anchored near Tanera Beg, the second largest island, beside a small yacht. Its skipper was sailing round Britain single-handed. He warned us not to anchor near submerged rocks at one end of the anchorage.

After dinner we went ashore and climbed to the top of Tanera Beg. A buzzard's nest overlooked the anchorage. We had magnificent views inland to the Sutherland mountains, and in the opposite direction we could see the Outer Hebrides.

Our port of call next morning was Ullapool on Loch Broom, where we had showers, shopped, and took on water. In the afternoon we had a fast sail to Loch Ewe and passed Gruinard Bay and its sinister island used for war gas experiments, and recently decontaminated from anthrax by drenching it with formaldehyde. We anchored overnight off the Island of Ewe.

On Friday morning we motored in a torrential downpour to Inverewe Gardens at the head of the loch. We walked round these magnificent gardens whose soil had come from the River

Liffey in Dublin as ship's ballast. The sun appeared at noon and a good wind gave us magnificent sailing round to Loch Gairloch. We anchored that night in Loch Shieldaig an inlet of Loch Gairloch, and returned the yacht to the charter company's moorings at Badachro on Saturday morning.

It had been a good cruise to interesting places with magnificent scenery and we were lucky to have had moderate winds on a coast exposed to the Atlantic, which could have been very stormy.

Replica of a birlinn

OYC mates on *Birlinn*

Chapter 10 – St. Kilda

Every Scottish yachtsman would like at some time to sail to St. Kilda, the archipelago forty-one miles out into the Atlantic to the west of the Outer Hebrides. They had been inhabited for 5,000 years continuously until they were evacuated at the islanders' request, in 1930. St. Kilda is presently owned by the National Trust for Scotland and occupied by NTS people plus technicians who man the radar station first used for tracking missiles from the rocket range on South Uist. They are a World Heritage Site and a National Trust Nature Reserve. They are managed jointly by the NTS, Scottish Heritage, and the MOD. When the original St. Kildans lived there, their only export was fulmar oil.

The anchorage at Village Bay on Hirta, the main island, is exposed from the south, and so is unsafe in southerly winds. I have been lucky to have visited it twice on OYT Scotland yachts.

On the first occasion we left Kyle of Lochalsh on 18 July 2000 in OYT Scotland's new seventy-foot vessel *Alba Venturer*. (The Ocean Youth Club had by then changed its name to Ocean Youth Trust.)

The professional skipper was Trevor Farrar, and I sailed as first mate. The nine young crew had been sponsored by five West of Scotland Rotary Clubs, including my own club, Barrhead.

Alba Venturer reached the Sound of Harris at dusk on Tuesday 18 July in a strong south-west wind. There was just enough light to see the guiding marks which help vessels to pass safely through its narrow channels. At dawn we arrived at Boreray, the impressive outlying island of the St. Kilda group which was covered by tens of thousands of nesting gannets.

The islands are all that remains of a huge extinct volcano which formed them sixty million years ago. The St. Kilda archipelago comprises seven large islands in two distinct groups about four and a half miles apart. The northern group are Boreray with its two large sea stacks, Stac Lee and Stac an Armin, the highest in the British Isles. The southern group are Hirta the main island, Dun which shelters Village Bay, Soay and Levenish, a sea stack south of Village Bay.

As we approached the main island of Hirta there were many different sea birds all around, - puffins, guillemots, great skuas, and fulmars. We anchored in Village Bay, and after introducing ourselves to the National Trust for Scotland warden Andy Robinson, we visited the shop in the military complex, and the fascinating museum housed in a renovated cottage. We were surprised at how small the habitable part of Hirta was. From the radar and radio masts on the top of the island we had splendid views of the other big islands of Soay, Dun and Boreray. Primitive looking Soay sheep, now feral, were everywhere, wandering around the many cleits (dry-stone cairn-shaped huts used for storing bird carcases). On our return to the ruined village we spotted several large St. Kilda wrens which live in the nooks and crannies of the old houses.

On Thursday morning we were off again, this time for Barra, in lovely sunny weather. We passed through the Sound of Pabbay and anchored in Vatersay Bay, which has a beautiful white beach. We had a barbecue ashore and a boisterous football match.

The next morning we sailed round to Castlebay on Barra to visit the swimming pool and the island's miniature airport. We watched a little plane land on the hard cockleshell beach for a quick turn-around of passengers. In the late evening we sailed on a beautiful moonlit night towards the island of Rum, catching a glimpse of the Northern Lights on the horizon.

We reached Rum on a hot Saturday morning and anchored off Kinloch Castle in Loch Scresort. There were a dozen yachts at anchor and a new pier was under construction. The boys had a great time swinging from the mast halyards and dropping into the sea. In the afternoon some of the crew visited the bizarre castle built by George Bullough the eccentric business magnate. Others climbed a nearby hill. Six of us walked the four miles across the island to Kilmory on the north side of Rum where we had a splendid view of the Cuillins on Skye. On the way we encountered a herd of large friendly Rum ponies and about fifty red deer including three stags with massive antlers. We saw many green and brown dragonflies, and were eaten alive by clegs – large horse flies.

On Saturday evening we had our third night-sail back to Kyle of Lochalsh in weak winds which eventually died away and we had to motor from dawn onwards. On the way we saw porpoises and otters. Once back at Kyle of Lochalsh a four hour clean-up prepared the boat for the next crew. We left by bus for Glasgow, well satisfied by our successful visit to St. Kilda.

My second visit to St. Kilda in August 2003 had not been planned when we left Ullapool in *Alba Venturer* bound for Taransay, the BBC castaway island at the western end of the Sound of Harris. The skipper this time was Tom Sage whom

I had met at Inverness airport, and drove to Ullapool. I was again sailing as first mate.

In fine weather, with our spectacular mizzen staysail with its blue AV monogram up, we crossed the Minch to anchor in Loch Shell on Harris.

When we passed through the Sound of Harris at mid-day the wind was north-westerly, just right for a landing on St. Kilda. The third mate, John, was a National Trust manager from the Lake District and was very keen to visit St. Kilda. The decision was taken to go there, and we abandoned Taransay for St. Kilda.

It became very hazy and sea mist became so dense that we had to use radar to reach Hirta that evening. We saw nothing of Hirta until we were actually in Village Bay when the leading lights appeared out of the mist dead ahead. We had difficulty getting the anchor to bite, and it took six attempts before we were secure. By the time we had supper were ready for our bunks.

Cloud level was very low when we went ashore and checked in with the NTS warden the next morning, but when the crew climbed up to the radar station, the masts were well above cloud level. There were tremendous views over the mist to Soay, and to the north, Stac an Armin and Boreray poked out of the fog bank.

We motored off early next morning in a flat calm to explore the northerly group of islands Boreray and its stacks, Stac an Armin and Stac Lee, which hold the largest gannetry in Europe with 45,000 birds. The St. Kildans used to visit Stac Lee in September to catch gugas or young gannets, for food. They had to lasso a peg on a cliff, then climb up the rope to land.

This was the Casting Off Point from which they threw the dead birds into the waiting boats. As we motored between the stacks we had close-up views of thousands of birds.

Stac an Armin is notorious as the place where St. Kildans killed the last great auk in the British Isles in 1840. It looked like a large guillemot or penguin and it is said they thought it was a witch. The bird became extinct when the last bird was killed in Iceland in 1844.

A fog bank beyond Stac an Armin now rolled in from the north. We turned the boat and headed back to Hirta. Later in the day we set off on our homeward voyage to Ullapool putting in to Lochmaddy and Loch Ewe on the way.

These were two memorable visits to St. Kilda and I am full of admiration for the St. Kildans who made a life for themselves in such a savage and remote place.

Beach barbecue at Vatersay Bay, Outer Hebrides

Stac Armin

On the top of Hirta

Chapter 11 – The Isle of Man

The Ocean Youth club had large yachts in six different locations in the UK, so I was spoiled for choice when I applied to sail on particular cruises. I sailed on many voyages on *Taikoo* the Scottish Area yacht based on the Clyde. It had been gifted to the OYC by Swire, the Hong Kong based shipping company and named after its shipyard there. I also sailed on OYC yachts based in Northern Ireland, Newcastle, East Anglia, and the South of England.

I had never sailed in Isle of Man waters so when the chance came to sail out of Douglas as first mate on *Francis Drake*, a sister ship to *Taikoo*, in July 1983, I took it. I spent an afternoon in Glasgow's Mitchell Library checking through the Admiralty Pilot Book for the Irish Sea, for navigational information about the Isle of Man area.

On reaching Douglas, by the ferry from Heysham, I joined *Francis Drake* to find that the crew were entirely drawn from the Isle of Man, and they all wanted to sail to Scotland. The skipper was David Crawford, and there was also an adult crew member on board who was an artist. She wanted some sailing experience before illustrating a book about the Mutiny on the Bounty. I had not realised that the mutineers had come from the Isle of Man.

We headed north the following morning, and put into Bangor in Belfast Lough for the night. Our next stop was at Campbeltown on the Kintyre Peninsula. The furthest north we reached was the secluded anchorage of Lowlandsman's Bay on Jura. On the way back to Douglas we stopped overnight at Carnlough Bay in Antrim.

In those days we depended on compass bearings on landmarks to determine our position. We could see the northern edge of the hills of the Isle of Man from some way off, but we were not looking at the northern tip of the island. Its low-lying coast was below the horizon.

Our last anchorage was at Strangford village at the narrows leading into Strangford Lough. An immense volume of tidal water surged through the channel, and we were intrigued at the unlikely courses sailed by a dinghy regatta fleet as the sideways movement of the boats in the tidal stream was considerable. On our way to Douglas next morning, with a favourable tide under us we shot out of the lough at high speed.

The cruise ended as usual with a big clean-up. The floorboards came up to be scrubbed on deck. The galley and heads were thoroughly cleaned and everything was made shipshape for the next crew to come aboard.

I returned to the Isle of Man many years later in 1997 when I was first mate on *Taikoo* with skipper Brian Eyres. *Taikoo* had spent that season sailing in English waters and we were bringing her home to Oban from Holyhead on Anglesey in Wales. The crew was an adult outdoor pursuits group from Rochdale.

We left Holyhead at 1700 on Monday 1 September in a gentle south-west wind and moderate sea. Number two jib, mizzen, and mizzen staysail got *Taikoo* to Port St. Mary on the southern tip of the Isle of Man at 0200 on Tuesday morning. She was then stormbound till the morning of Wednesday 3 September, sheltering from a south-east gale behind the high harbour wall. With a springs tidal range of over five metres, the spray was coming right over the wall at high water. The heavy anchor warp and nine other lines kept the boat secure to the wall and the sea staff kept an anchor watch throughout the night.

At breakfast next morning we were shocked to learn that Diana, Princess of Wales had been killed in a car crash in Paris on Sunday 31 August.

Gale warnings for the Irish Sea were in force for several days but a window in the weather was forecast for Wednesday morning. As soon as the cold front had passed through and the wind had veered into the southwest, *Taikoo* was off in bright sunshine, butting into the still rough seas under engine as far as Chicken Rock Light.

Once we could bear away for Northern Ireland the wind dropped to give comfortable sailing in moderate to fresh wind, culminating in a spanking reach in the dark into Belfast Lough. We tied up at Bangor at 0245 on Thursday morning.

Kay the leader of the outdoor pursuits group had an injured knee and had to be hoisted up on to the harbour wall for a hospital check-up. When she returned she was on crutches. We became adept at hoisting her on and off the vessel throughout the trip.

Gale warnings were still in force but while the wind remained in the south and the sea state was moderate, we were anxious to get off, so we left Bangor at 1110 the same day. Keeping into the lee of the Irish shore as far as Rathlin in a fresh breeze, we had expected to find stronger winds offshore, but in fact the wind dropped to a light breeze and veered to the southwest.

As we sailed up the Sound of Jura, heavy showers reduced

visibility, and the wind gradually increased to a near gale. The mizzen staysail was dropped at dusk and the double-reefed mainsail came down at 0045 leaving us with only the number three jib, and still doing eight knots as we sped northwards.

In the early hours of Friday morning we caught the tide through the Sound of Luing, carefully watching the radar screen, and noting the light sector changes as we passed between the lights of Fladda and Dubh Sgeir. Avoiding the rocks off Easdale we made our way into the Sound of Insh, then as day broke we entered the Sound of Kerrera. We tied up to a heavy mooring buoy behind Heather Island at 0635 and as we were all exhausted, crashed out for a couple of hours before breakfast.

The usual mammoth end of voyage clean-up then began and a tidy *Francis Drake* was brought into the North Pier at Oban at mid-day.

OYC ketch *Francis Drake*

OYC ketch *Taikoo*

Chapter 12 – Round Jura to Carrickfergus

Doug our skipper tossed Sammy over the side and shouted: 'Man overboard!'

John the second mate, spun *Taikoo*'s wheel to bear away on to a reach as we began the approved RYA man-overboard drill on Loch Ryan, on the morning of Sunday 3 July 1988. Sammy was our practice dummy, resplendent in his yellow OYC Henri Lloyd oilskins. Lookouts kept a close eye on him as we went about, dropping the genoa to the deck before luffing up alongside him.

I, the first mate, had the boathook out and caught Sammy by his anorak hood, but the water had now filled the dummy's clothing making him as heavy as a real man. I found it impossible to lift him back on board.

The skipper had meantime passed the mizzen staysail halyard through a snatch block clipped to the deck, and on to the large cockpit winch. Fiona the bosun, in a bosun's chair, was shackled to the business end of the halyard and hung like a racing-dinghy crew on a trapeze, over the side. She held a helicopter strop ready to pass over Sammy's head and shoulders. She lassoed him deftly as we passed and then Sammy and Fiona were both winched safely on board.

Patricia, the trainee mate and I then each had a go on the wheel. After half an hour's practice, Doug felt ready for us to set off for Rathlin Island just off the Irish coast, our first day's destination on an OYC cruise which would take us round

Jura and finish at Carrickfergus on Belfast Lough at the end of the week.

The skipper, mates, bosun and crew had gathered on *Taikoo* at Stranraer's railway pier the previous evening. We were sixteen in all. Doug Hinge, the relief skipper, was giving the regular skipper Anna Stratton a break. He had not sailed in Scottish waters before and was keen to take *Taikoo* through the Gulf of Corryvreckan between the north end of Jura and Scarba. A transatlantic sailor, he was young, cheerful, and reassuringly confident.

Doug and John Spiers the second mate were strangers to me, but I had met Patricia Rooney at our winter mates' training sessions. Fiona Emery the bosun was an English sixth-former who was spending a month on the boat on a working holiday keeping everything shipshape and providing a valuable link between the young crew and the adult afterguard.

The crew was the usual mixture of young people on an OYC cruise, from varied backgrounds. The three Peters, Peter Wells, Peter Webster, and Peter Dougan were in their late teens and had some dinghy sailing experience. Mark Frame, the youngest at fifteen, was sponsored by the Social Work Department. Karin Bursell was a Swedish girl. The rest of the crew were an older group of YTS trainees led by a high spirited and popular twenty-year-old, George Gibson. They all worked together in the offices of Inverclyde District Council in Greenock. They were Heather Dougan, David Speck, Jennifer Law, John Young and Loraine Murray.

In fine sunny weather under genoa, staysail, main, and mizzen we reached across to the Irish coast in a brisk north-easterly. The Mull of Kintyre dominated the northern horizon as we approached Rathlin Island and Fair Head.

The wind backed as we came up to Rathlin, so we hardened in the sheets and beat towards Fair Head. The powerful tidal stream sluicing through Rathlin Sound gave us a useful lee bow push as we crabbed our way into the sound. The roar of the overfalls in the McDonnell Race could be heard to starboard and in the low evening sunlight a line of broken water was clearly visible.

To ensure that the tide would not carry us too far into the sound, we sailed down a useful transit line keeping Rue Point, the south-east end of Rathlin, and Benbane Head beyond it, in line. As soon as Rue Point had been passed we slipped out of the tidal stream into the sheltered waters of Church Bay.

Rathlin is shaped like a right-angled boomerang. Its two arms of low white cliffs form the quiet anchorage of Church Bay, sheltering boats perfectly from the north. Twice we failed to dig in the anchor off the white cliffs to the west of the tiny village, possibly due to heavy kelp on the bottom. A more likely spot with a shoaling bottom off the eastern side of the bay was selected and she finally held there. With a sigh of relief, the crew went below for supper, tired by hauling the anchor up twice without the aid of an anchor winch.

Later, the dinghy was hoisted over the side on the main topping lift, and I took a shore party over to the little village. The pub was clearly the focus of island life, but the locals were not very communicative. This quiet tenor of island life was shattered however by an almighty crash outside! The pub emptied instantly. One of the island's battered cars had been involved in a collision. Voices were raised. The car roared off. The drinkers returned, and without a word, resumed their Guinness drinks in laid-back silence!

As a boy I had read how Robert the Bruce had exiled himself to Rathlin when his fortunes were low. He is said to have seen the legendary spider whose persistence in making a web inspired him to continue with his struggle for Scottish independence. The island had captured my imagination then; it has a romantic mysterious air today, but the locals don't tell you much.

There was a bit of sea mist as we left on Monday 4 July bound for West Loch Tarbert on the Kintyre peninsula. The wind was light and variable and we were soon becalmed. We motored north for a while to avoid being swept past the Mull of Kintyre by the tide. As the sun rose, the north-east wind reappeared and we beat up the Sound of Jura giving Cath Sgeir on the west side of Gigha a good offing.

The entrance to West Loch Tarbert was not immediately obvious but a fleet of trimly painted prawn boats swept out to show us the way in. We dropped all sails but the mizzen and motored carefully up the loch past Kennacraig to the old pier at the head of the loch as a gale warning had been received over the radio. There was just enough depth for *Taikoo* at low water.

At 0720 on Tuesday 5 July we slipped our warps and moved off to make room for the returning prawn boats. They made a fine sight in the morning sun as the flotilla approached in line astern, bow waves foaming. A Spanish articulated refrigerated lorry awaited their catch at the pier.

The threatened gale had come to nothing and in very light airs the tide slowly drifted us up the Sound of Jura. Visibility deteriorated in a fine drizzle, A chicken dinner raised morale, and we dropped the sails and motored up Loch Craignish with its avenue of islands to Ardfern.

We went ashore that evening to the pub at Ardfern and I bumped into George Rich who had been the OYC Scottish Area Manager when I first sailed with the OYC. I told him about our current cruise and he asked where we were bound for next. I said we were going through the Gulf of Corryvreckan the next day then sailing south to Ireland. George hesitated then said,

'I would never under any circumstances go through the Corryvreckan.'

I remembered scenes from the 1945 Powell and Pressburger film, *I Know Where I'm Going*, depicting the giant whirlpool in all its fury. I also remembered that in 1947, George Orwell, who had been writing *1984* while living in a cottage on Jura, had nearly drowned there when his dinghy capsized. He had misjudged the timing of the tides. We would have to be very careful tomorrow.

The time of the turn of the tide at the Gulf of Corryvreckan determined our departure time from Ardfern as it is much safer to pass through the gulf at slack water. We planned to leave at 1300, so spent the morning cleaning ship, having showers ashore, shopping, and taking photographs from the hillside overlooking this beautiful yacht haven.

The notorious Corryreckan whirlpool is caused by the tidal stream striking a submerged pinnacle at the western end of the channel. When we motored past the spot, the water boiled and gurgled and swung us about a bit, but we emerged from the gulf unscathed.

A strong westerly wind now blew us south. We reefed down and soon *Taikoo* was reaching at high speed down the west coast of Jura. Young Mark nearly took a header over the side when he tripped over a deck fitting as he skipped about the deck. Thankfully, he was tethered to the boat by his safety harness and I caught him in time. I had a few choice words to say to him. OYC mates have to keep alert.

By the time my watch came on duty at 0400 on Thursday 7 July the wind had come up again from the west and it was a cold, grey, and damp start to the day. Rathlin and Fair Head eventually loomed out of the mist, the wind backing into the north-east, and we beat our way along the Irish coast past the Maidens.

At 1600 we tied up at Bangor where we were entertained by OYC Northern Ireland members at the yacht club. On the Friday morning we motored over to Carrickfergus Marina for our crew change. It had been a happy cruise of 235 miles and we had enjoyed sailing together in these spectacular waters of the West Coast of Scotland and Northern Ireland.

Taikoo at Ardfern

Taikoo on passage north

Taikoo beating to windward near the Faroe Islands

Chapter 13 – The Faroe Islands

The tidal atlas for the Faroe Islands has this extract from an old report on a steamship's experience in a strong tidal stream:

'A Happening East of Sandoy'

'In the middle of the twenties it happened that a steamship under way to Iceland touched at Torshavn for a little repair.

Leaving Torshavn, the captain decided that the ship was too large to turn to starboard over at the south end of Stremoy, so he would go east of Sandoy, and well clear there, he would turn to starboard over. That the tidal circumstances were shown in Chart No. 3 in 'Tidal Current around the Faroe Islands' he did not know anything about.

The weather was fine, a little breeze from the south-east, but the south-east going current was in very bad spirit, and before the captain thought about it, they were in a very critical situation.

In the afternoon, the steamer again arrived in Torshavn, but this time without funnel and boats. The ship was about 4,000 tons deadweight, the engine amidships as the custom of the time was.'

I was reading this enlightening account on *Taikoo*, moored at Kyle of Lochalsh on Sunday 2 July 1989, in preparation for an OYC cruise to the Faroe Islands. These islands, which lie between Shetland and Iceland, have a similar relationship to Denmark as the Isle of Man does to the UK.

I browsed through the pages of the tidal atlas, each page giving a graphic hourly picture of direction and speed of tidal streams along coastlines and through sounds. Every page had red danger areas like a spattering of blood drops. Ships were advised not to enter any of these areas of turbulence. Scottish waters have areas of fast tidal races like the Kyle of Lochalsh or the Gulf of Corryvreckan, but these areas in the Faroes were on an altogether different scale.

Raised voices and a clattering of feet on the deck above, marked the arrival of our crew who were aged fifteen to twenty-four. The adults on board, or afterguard, were very experienced; as well as skipper Anna Stratton, it included a supernumerary, Pete Bentley who was also a relief skipper and a short-wave radio ham. The mates were myself as first mate, Thea Groves, an instructor at Benmore Outdoor Education Centre near Dunoon whom I had known for some time, and Steve, a yacht designer from McGruer's on the Clyde. The bosun was Jamie, and there were twelve young crew members. Every berth was filled.

We got to know each other that evening and after a meal and a safety briefing, we turned in for an early start the next day.

It was a fine sunny morning as we left Kyle of Lochalsh, sailing up the Inner Sound between Skye and the mainland. We had a man-overboard drill, practising winching the recovered man from the sea with a hoist from a mast halyard. The mizzen staysail gave us a knot or two more and we sped northwards. A three-watch system was set up with three hours on and six hours off.

We made our point of departure the Crowlin Islands, and marked our position on the chart every hour, allowing for tidal flow. Navigational aids were a Decca Navigator radio beacon system, and sextants for sun sights. No stars were seen on this summer trip in northerly latitudes. We also carried an EPIRB, - Emergency Position Indicating Radio Beacon, which if activated would give our position to passing airliners.

Our route took us past the Butt of Lewis and between Sula Sgeir and Rona. As we sailed north, we saw black and white dolphins, gannets and puffins. The hours of darkness were short and on Tuesday morning a whale was spotted, then a Faroese fishing boat. It was a drizzly morning but gradually the distinctive pyramidal-shaped Faroese mountains emerged from the mist, the sun came out, and we took fixes from local radio beacons.

We confirmed our position with fixes off Litla Dimun and Stora Dimun to the east of a tidal disturbance. As we approached the little capital Torshavn (population 15,000), many ferry-boats appeared. A north wind cleared the fog and it was cold, with exceptional visibility. Spectacular islands were all around.

The Faroes population in 1989 was 46,000 and its first parliament was set up 1,000 years ago. Faroese is closely related to Icelandic, and Danish and English are also spoken. The Faroes economy is entirely dependent on fishing. It has its own flag and bank notes. The average summer temperature is eleven degrees C and average winter temperature is three degrees C. There are nineteen and a half hours of daylight at midsummer and five hours of daylight at midwinter. At midnight we could read a newspaper on deck.

The marina at Torshavn where we tied up was full of fishing boats, and a rowing race was ending there as we arrived.

Rowing in distinctive double- ended boats is the national sport.

Our arrival created great local interest as there was no tradition there of pleasure sailing, but foreign yachts called there each summer. We had many visitors, including a Scottish artist from Gourock. He told us that the Faroese were very well off. Deck hands on Greenland trawlers were earning £1,000 a week. There were no pubs, but each Faroese had a generous weekly personal alcohol ration of a litre of spirits and a case of beer!

We also learned that our arrival had coincided with the World Island Games being hosted by the Faroe Islands that year.

Scandinavian influence was evident in a new double-ended boat being built at Torshavn, with its high prow and stern posts. An outboard motor could be mounted on an open box in its hull.

After an early morning swim and sauna at the swimming pool at Torshavn, and a morning of sightseeing, we left Torshavn on Wednesday 5 July sailing south of Nolsoy and then northwards to the fishing village of Fuglafjordur on Eysturoy.

It was a cold overcast afternoon with a strong breeze obliging us to change down to a smaller headsail. We sailed into a dense fog bank and the wind dropped. We could not see our bows from the wheel in the cockpit. Engine and radar were switched on as we entered Leirvik Fjord.

The echo of a ship appeared on the radar screen dead ahead. We took avoiding action by turning to starboard. The other boat turned to its port and was still dead ahead. We turned to port. The other boat turned to its starboard. It was still dead ahead. Our chart gave the explanation. We were dodging our own echo reflected off an overhead cable slung across the fjord, which was acting like a radio mirror.

The radar picture started to spin around. At first the helmsman was blamed, but then we noticed ripples in the water. We were in a powerful tidal stream. At that instant the fog lifted, we had sudden sunshine, and excellent visibility. We found ourselves being carried towards the side of the fjord. Quick avoiding action took us clear and soon we were tied up alongside the fish factory at Fuglafjordur. After supper we had a sing-song led by Steve on his guitar.

The next morning Thursday 6 July we cleaned the boat, then went ashore to have a look around. One group explored the village while another, myself included, climbed Borgin, the hill overlooking Fuglafjordur.

We climbed up through meadows of wild flowers, grazed by small Faroese sheep, which were similar to the black Soay sheep I had seen on St. Kilda, but these were white with black spots. The hills all around had pyramidal profiles and were composed of layers of lava and volcanic ash. At the summit of Borgin we found rock imbedded with green crystals.

Before leaving Fuglafjordur we had a tour of its very modern fish factory where fish were automatically gutted, boned and deep frozen into blocks for export all over the world, even reaching Australia. Ninety-seven per cent of the Faroes population were employed in the fish industry.

In the late afternoon we continued north up Djupini Sound, beating fast into a strong wind. We changed down our headsail just as we reached a tidal race again. *Taikoo* accelerated rapidly. We swooped over huge standing waves fifteen to twenty feet high with a wavelength of about a hundred feet. The wave height got bigger and bigger and just as we wondered how much higher it would grow, we sailed clear into smoother water.

Leaving Djupini Sound we turned westwards to the little village of Eidi on Eysturoy for an overnight stop. Not a soul was in sight when we arrived. It was utterly silent, but signs of human activity were evident in the racks of cod hung out to dry in the wind.

Eidi was a pleasant little village with a new harbour wall and an attractive hotel which was being occupied by tourists from Scotland. We met a tour operator, David Paterson from Culross in Fife, who organised package holidays to the Faroes.

On Friday 7 July we left Eidi, travelling eastwards along a rugged coast of islands and sounds. We passed two impressive sea stacks off Eidi known as the Giant and the Witch. They are said to have been sent by Icelanders to tow the Faroes to Iceland but they were thwarted by a Faroese wizard who turned them into stone.

We had an excellent view of the highest sea cliff in Europe, the Enniberg towering above us in a sheer vertical fall of 2000 feet. An arctic skua with long trailing feathers soared next the cliff in the updraught.

Our last overnight stop in the Faroes was at anchor in Vidvik, a deep fjord on the island of Vidoy. Looking ashore from *Taikoo*'s anchorage, I counted forty layers of lava from sea level to mountain top beyond the beach.

We had visitors here. A father, his daughter, and another girl, approached us in a little fishing boat shaped like a tiny Viking longship. We invited them on board for tea and biscuits. They were fascinated by *Taikoo*, and intrigued by our ocean-going equipment.

Pete our relief skipper had brought his high frequency transceiver with him. He now set it up and contacted another radio ham in the Ukraine. He had difficulty explaining to him who we were and where we were.

We went ashore to explore this apparently deserted island. At about midnight we had a sing-song around a campfire, then in turn we raced the dinghy back to *Taikoo* in three teams.

At 0100 on Saturday 8 July we began our voyage home to the Shetland Islands, passing between Fugloy and Svinoy, helped on our way by another tidal stream. By 0200 the sky lightened up. There was no darkness at all. Lighthouses here are switched off for the summer months. It was a quiet sail with light winds and we were visited by a pod of dolphins, swimming so close to the boat that we could look down on their blowholes.

The next day, Sunday 9 July, we could see the distinctive outline of Foula, the most westerly of the Shetland Islands from many miles off. Gradually, more islands appeared.

We reached Sumburgh Head, slowly sailing against the Sumburgh Roost, a strong tidal race off the south end of the Shetlands beside Jarlshof the stone- age village.

A very pleasant sunny evening finished off our cruise, sailing past the impressive Iron Age Broch of Mousa. We were welcomed by seals as we ghosted up the Sound of Bressay to Lerwick, which we reached at 0100 on Monday 12 July. Within minutes of berthing, Customs had cleared us and the voyage was over.

The next evening, we handed over to a new crew and came home to Aberdeen by the car ferry. It had been a wonderful trip with a very happy crew, all glad of this chance to participate in our expedition to the Faroe Islands.

Taikoo at Vidvik on Vidoy

Chapter 14 – Norway

I had the chance in July 1991 to sail to Norway as first mate on *James Cook*, the OYC north-east area ketch based on the Tyne. It was a Shipwright 70 Class steel-hulled vessel built by British Shipbuilders on Tyneside and commissioned in 1986.

The previous September I had sailed on *James Cook* on a familiarisation weekend with an all-adults cruise out of Hartlepool, and got to know its skipper Ed Bradshaw. I was amazed that this very competent skipper was seasick every time he went to sea, but it didn't last long, and he quickly shrugged it off.

Ed Bradshaw was again the skipper when we set off from Blyth on our way to Bergen in Norway on Sunday 7 July 1991. I was the first mate, and the second mate was Simon Bryan-Smith. We also had a trainee mate, Sarah Watt, whom I had sailed with when she was the bosun on the OYC flagship *Duet* on the Oban to Aberdeen leg of the OYC Round Britain Rally in July 1985.

It was warm and humid, as we motored in calm weather to North Shields where we carried out man overboard drill. This had to be abandoned when thick mist developed and we had to wait at North Shields till it lifted around mid-day on Monday 8 July. We finally got under away at 1400 in a south-east fresh breeze.

We sailed in a south-west gentle wind overnight but in the afternoon of Tuesday 9 July the wind backed to south-south-west and rose to a strong breeze. We dropped the main and from 1800 onwards sailed under yankee jib alone, running before the wind. During the day of Wednesday 10 July the wind veered through south-west to north-west giving very good reaching conditions and fast sailing.

Our Decca radio location system was faulty and our estimated chart position obviously overestimated our progress, as it reached land before the boat did! At 1600 we saw what was obviously the south coast of Norway ahead. We realised that we had been driven well to the south of our intended course to Bergen.

Another problem to be faced was that our coastal charts were all covering the Bergen area, not this coastline ahead. It was difficult to identify where we were. We passed a red and white striped lighthouse on our starboard side and entered a deep wide fjord, which branched inside its entrance.

Red and green navigational buoys marked a channel, which we followed to an attractive little red-roofed village, flying Norwegian flags, and tied up to its small jetty. I jumped ashore and knocked at the door of the nearest house and politely asked the housewife who opened the door where we were! Andabeloy on Flekkefjord was her reply. We had logged 341 miles from North Shields.

We learned later that the fjord we had entered from the sea was Listafjord which branched into its western arm Flekkefjord and its eastern arm Fedafjord.

It was essential that we now bought charts for the south coast of Norway. We could do this at the town of Flekkefjord, which lay at the head of that fjord, which we visited the following day.

While I went ashore with the young crew to buy the charts, the skipper, bosun and other mates opened up the central water tank. We had noticed on the crossing that the ship's water had a slightly earthy taste. The tank had been contaminated with brown algae. After it had been thoroughly cleaned, it was closed up, refilled with fresh water, and the work party had welcome showers at the Hotel Maritim.

We left for Kristiansand on the south coast of Norway on Saturday 13 July, beating out of Listafjord, then turning east, reaching along the Norwegian coast past the southernmost point of Norway. The charts I had bought at Flykkefjord were Norwegian yachtsmen's charts giving excellent coverage of the rocky coast. We reached Kristiansand in a torrential downpour and tied up in the western harbour.

The following day we set off southwards at 1430 bound for Esbjerg in Denmark. It was a very bright sunny afternoon with very strong winds and heavy seas, which broke over our bows. At nightfall we dropped the main and sailed through the night under number three genoa and mizzen sail. Monday morning 15 July was wet and miserable with very poor visibility.

Our mood was lifted around mid-day when we were visited by a dolphin. It surfaced behind the boat, then played in our bow wave before leaping twice completely out of the water.

As we approached Esbjerg under sail around 0100 on Tuesday 16 July, we spotted the lights of a small coaster on a collision course with us, and had to take avoiding action although we had right of way.

Esbjerg has sandbanks offshore and we motored along a well-lit dredged channel to the harbour where we tied up at 0140. After a rather late (!) dinner of chili con carne the afterguard went for a walk, returning at dawn at 0300 just as the birds began their dawn chorus.

On Wednesday 17 July we left Esbjerg at 0730 in a fresh breeze and sailed out along the well-marked shipping channel. Once clear of the sand banks we hoisted our number one jib, main and mizzen, and set off on the starboard tack. The wind was expected to go southerly in due course, which would help as to reach the Humber.

On Thursday 18 July the sky started to cloud over at 0900 and we were startled by three loud sonic booms from two jet fighter aircraft overhead. We watched them practise a dogfight as they chased each other in ever decreasing circles.

Around 1000 the wind began to freshen. We stopped the engine and re-hoisted the jib. Soon we were cracking along at eight knots. At mid-day we crossed a busy shipping lane north of the Frisian Islands. The crew were relaxed and we made a pasta lunch while we listened to classical music on a tape brought by Tom Ball one of the crew who was an aspiring classical pianist.

By the evening the wind had piped up even more and we had an exciting fast night sail, still beating into the wind. We had the midnight to 0300 watch and passed very close to gas rigs at the end of our watch.

From 0900-1200 on Friday 19 July we had fast sailing in a strong breeze but by 1500 we were becalmed, and the skipper decided to motor the last eighty miles to Hull to meet his deadlines. We reached Spurn Point at the mouth of the Humber at 1800.

I phoned Gill by radio link call and learned that our grandson Luke had been born to Ruth and Martin on Wednesday 17 July 1991. Weight, seven pounds twelve ounces. I felt very happy as we motored up the Humber to Hull Marina.

On Saturday we had the usual massive boat clean-up prior to a scheduled crew change. In the evening we celebrated Luke's birthday with a splendid beef casserole cooked by Sarah, followed by creamed rice, and a birthday cake I had bought in Hull. As we finished the evening ashore at a quiet pub, we were serenaded by a jazz band at the quayside, part of the festivities to mark the British Powerboat Championships being held on the Humber.

Next day I travelled back to Blyth to collect my car. The last leg of this journey was by taxi from Whitley Bay to Blyth. I told the taxi driver of our voyage to Norway and back, and I gave him an OYC brochure as he was very keen to join the OYC since he was still under twenty-five.

At the head of Fedafjord

Tom Ball helming *James Cook*

Chapter 15 – Greece

My sister Morag Cameron and her partner Guy Cotsell were keen to sail in the Cyclades islands in Greece. Morag was an administrator with the Australian Gas Association and Guy was a retired Australian diplomat. They asked me if I could organise a cruise there in July 1993. They lived in Australia and we agreed we could meet up in Athens.

Gerry Fretz, a retired training air captain who had managed an airline pilot training school at Prestwick Airport agreed to be my first mate. I had sailed with Gerry on the Firth of Clyde on his Moody 31 yacht *Southern Comfort*, with another friend Ian Dryburgh, a building contractor, who also agreed to join our crew. Jerry and Ian had sailed together in 1992 in Turkey.

I looked at the yacht chartering advertisements in *Yachting Monthly* and approached a company which specialised in Greece. They had a yacht available, which was based at Naoussa on the island of Paros. They accepted my RYA Yachtmaster qualification as proof of my competence as a skipper, and I chartered the yacht for a week.

Now I needed to find out as much as I could about the Cyclades. I had heard about the spectacular island of Santorini, to the south of Paros, so that would be on our itinerary. Other smaller islands in the Southern Cyclades looked promising, and I planned a cruise starting on Paros, then on to Iraklia, Thira (Santorini), Amorgos, Schinoussa, Naxos, and back to Paros.

Gerry, Ian and I flew to Athens on 3 July 1993 and met

Morag and Guy at a small hotel in central Athens, which had been recommended to Guy by his Australian friends. The next morning, we flew to Paros, about a hundred miles south-east of Athens in a small Dornier plane which gave us an excellent view of the islands.

We arrived by taxi at Piso Livadi, where we were to join the yacht. It was nowhere to be seen. I phoned the boat's Greek agent from a local hotel, and was told that he was still in Athens, but the yacht was being delivered to Naoussa on the north coast of Paros. After lunch in a local restaurant we drove by taxi to Naoussa. At the harbour we found our boat, not the yacht we had booked, but a similar Jeanneau Sunrise 34 called *Anpava*.

The Greek delivery skipper showed us over the boat and asked us to return it to Naoussa, or Parikia the island's capital in a week's time. After he had gone, I realised that I had not been asked for the usual security deposit to cover any damage we might do to the boat during our cruise.

Naoussa was an attractive fishing village with lots of quayside tavernas selling fresh seafood like octopus, swordfish and red mullet. We ate well that evening and the lean cats roaming the harbour streets dined well too from any food that fell off the tables.

It was a pleasant sunny day next morning as we sailed round the north-east corner of Paros and down the straits between Paros and Naxos. Morag remarked what a pity it was that dolphins were not seen now so frequently in the Aegean. Dead on cue a school of about twenty dolphins appeared off the port bow and entertained us by 'buzzing' the yacht from either side for fifteen minutes. This was the only time we saw dolphins. It was idyllic sailing with lots of sun and seas which were an unbelievable royal blue colour.

We put into Agios Giorgos on the tiny island of Iraklia, to the south of Naxos. Only one other yacht was tied up at the short quay. From our deck we watched island life, enlivened by the arrival of the ferry Skipolitos which we were to see frequently on our tour of the islands. On the nearby beach local people were tidying up the sand for the arrival of visitors. We had an excellent meal of fresh fish that evening at the quayside taverna and at midnight the ferry arrived again ablaze with light, like a spaceship in the darkness.

The next day we sailed south to Santorini or Thira. Around 3,000 B.C. a cataclysmic volcanic eruption caused the centre of the island to collapse into a huge crater. The resultant tsunami is thought to have destroyed the Minoan cities on Crete to the south. As the eruption was about four times bigger than the eruption of Krakatoa in 1883, it is not surprising that this event is possibly the origin of the story of the lost city of Atlantis. The present towns on Santorini are all perched on the lip of this crater which has two breaks in it, so you actually sail into a crater about two miles across.

High onshore winds meant that we could not tie up at the main town of Santorini and we had to anchor off a sheltered black sandy beach beside Akrotiri lighthouse. We went ashore briefly that evening to an island made of volcanic ash which looked very desolate but which grew excellent vines.

We left at dawn the next morning, retracing our course across the crater. We passed two new small islands emerging from the hot lava coming out of the submerged crater. Ominous bubbles of hot volcanic gas gurgled around our hull.

Our course north-east took us past the barren island of Anhydrous, from its name presumably waterless. It was hot, humid and hazy as we approached the island of Amorgos. We got ready to moor the yacht at the quay at Katapola.

The harbourmaster signalled to us to motor in backwards, dropping the anchor over the bow to slow us down as we approached the quay, and finally to tie up stern first with two lines in the Mediterranean manner. Not easy, but we managed the manoeuvre first go. We asked a smartly dressed man in a white shirt to take our lines but he refused. Trust us to ask the local drunk. However, the harbourmaster, also very smart in a white uniform with gold badges, nonchalantly took up our lines and tied us up at the quay.

Another yacht had less success. It was a battered old boat owned by an ancient English couple. They came in bow first at great speed and amid much cursing and swearing, they hit a large Greek yacht. They backed off and tried again, only to hit the same boat a second time. This caused great amusement to everyone else. We learned later that their boat had been sailed around, not across, the Bay of Biscay and was bound for the Middle East.

Katapola was a lively little town with good shops and many tavernas. Donkeys were in regular use as well as more modern transport. We had showers in the hotel, and a good seafood dinner in a taverna in the evening.

We were short of water but could not get any at the quay-side as the farmer who now and then turned on the water for boats, was late. We decided to sail on and fill up at our next port of call.

The little islands to the south of Naxos were attractive and the sandy shallows between the islands were coloured deep blue and turquoise. We threaded our way between the islets in light airs and arrived at Mersini, a tiny harbour on the island of Schinoussa. This was our favourite island of all those we visited.

The main village of Hora was situated about a mile inland from the harbour, to hide it from pirates in the old days. We had an evening stroll to the village while our evening meal was being prepared at the harbour taverna. We were overtaken by a tractor pulling an empty trailer. Its driver gave us a lift to the village. It was a beautiful old hilltop village with good views to the neighbouring islands. We were of great interest to the smiling villagers as this island did not get many visitors, and we were quite touched when an old lady presented each of us with a rose!

The taverna at Mersini had prepared a very good seafood meal for us and hungry cats under the table rubbed against our legs hoping for fish titbits. We returned for breakfast next morning and watched a herd of goats pass by, then a little donkey carrying drums for water arrived. It carried water from the harbour well up to the village. We managed to get some of this well water too but kept it in a drum as it was slightly brackish.

Our next stop was the island of Naxos. We anchored for lunch and a swim near Aia Anna. To get back to Naoussa we now had a hard beat in the sound between Naxos and Paros as the Meltemi, the north wind, gathered force. Off Cape Kouroupas we had to put two reefs in the mainsail and rolled up the headsail to show only two metres of sail. Suddenly, the sail ripped horizontally across its breadth and we limped across the straits under reefed mainsail and engine to Piso

Livadi where we were to have picked up the boat at the start of the cruise.

I phoned the charter company in London and we agreed to leave the yacht at Piso Livadi as we could not get the sail repaired and we had no spare headsail. Our last day of the charter was spent on the beach at Piso Livadi.

Next morning, we flew to Athens where we went our separate ways. Morag and Guy visited our sister Flora who lived in Ceraso in southern Italy, Gerry stayed for a few days in Athens, and Ian and I returned to London and on to Glasgow.

Negotiations with the charter company later resulted in our getting a refund of the cost of the lost day's sailing. It had been a great experience and we had enjoyed the sun and sailing in the Cyclades.

Arriving at Santorini

Dolphin

Crew of *Anpova*
Left to right, Ian Dryburgh, Morag, Gerry, Ian, and Guy

Chapter 16 – Zeeland

As a boy, I had enjoyed Arthur Ransome's children's novel, *We Didn't Mean to Go to Sea*, about an unexpected voyage to Flushing (Vlissingen) in the Netherlands by the Walker children. When I learned that the OYC East Area boat *Spirit of Boadicea* planned to make the same trip from Ipswich to Flushing from 2-8 July 1994, I quickly signed on for the voyage as first mate. *Boadicea* was an OYC Robert Clark ketch and a sister ship *Taikoo*.

The skipper was Alan Fraser, an extrovert character who had supported Holland in the World Football Cup. The second mate Ian was a policeman under assessment for first mate during the trip. The other second mate Jack was retired and over seventy. We also had a trainee mate, Nigel who was a student. Chris was the bosun, a young woman who wanted to make her career in the yachting world.

We had a crew of eleven young people on board. Nine girls were from a boarding school in Harrogate, hoping to have the cruise accepted as part of their assessment for the Duke of Edinburgh's Award, and lastly, a boy and a girl from Ipswich. The Harrogate girls were rather immature and giggly, and fond of making practical jokes on each other. Alan had strong reservations about them.

The night before we set off, we did the usual briefing, fire drill, checked that the new fire hose was working, issued safety belts and harnesses and introduced the crew to the sails and rigging. In the morning of Sunday 3 July, we motored out of Ipswich Harbour through the lock gate into the River Orwell, got the sails up and practised handling the boat under sail. We made our way down river past Thames sailing barges, now pleasure boats, tied up after a rally at Pin Mill.

We left Harwich by the buoyed channel taking us north of the sandbanks. At mid-day, we sailed into a bank of really thick fog. As a lot of shipping was about, we dropped the sails, put on the engine and started to sound our foghorn. We could feel the wash from invisible ships around us and could hear their engines. Under radar we crept over a sandbank bedside Rough Tower and dropped anchor where ships would not come near.

Two hours later, sunshine suddenly burst through the fog and we were able to set off for the Netherlands. It was an easy crossing. We altered course to avoid one or two ships in the night, but there were many buoys and lightships to guide us past the sandbanks. About 0400 next morning we arrived at the Kaloo Buoy off Vlissingen where pilot boats wait for their customers. We followed a marked channel close inshore to Vlissingen.

The town lies on the island of Walcheren on the north side of the Westerschelde estuary in an area known as Zeeland. It has dams between the islands to control storm surges and river spates, rather like the Thames Barrier. Behind these dams there are inland waterways full of yachts, in a very attractive recreational area.

We entered the sea lock to the harbour, then motored along the Walcheren Canal to Middelburg the capital of the island, a beautiful moated medieval town, where we tied up for the night. After dinner we had a pleasant evening at the local yacht club where some friendly Dutch yachtsmen introduced us to Genever, the Dutch juniper-based liqueur.

The following day, Tuesday 5 July, we sailed into Veresemeer, the passage between Walcheren and the island of Noordbeveland, wending our way through fishing boats and yachts into the Oosterschelde estuary. We made our way under the Zeeland Bridge, which takes a motorway over the Oosterschelde and entered the harbour of Zieriksee, another fortified medieval town which was besieged by Spanish troops in 1575.

On Wednesday 6 July we retraced our steps to Walcheren, passing many yachts and barges fitted with leeboards to stop sideways drift, rather than the deep keels which were familiar to us.

Our last night in the Netherlands was spent at Vere at the northern end of the Walcheren Canal. This was a pleasant little town with trading associations with Scotland. In 1444 Wolfert van Brossele, Lord of Vere married Princess Mary, one of the six daughters of James I of Scotland. This led to a wool trade and special privileges for Scottish merchants in Vere who stayed there until Napoleon's troops arrived in 1795.

The wind rose as we left Vlissingen on Thursday 7 July and we quickly put a reef in the main. Most of the crew were seasick as wind against tide made the sea choppy. So few of the crew were fit to stand a watch, that for most of the voyage home, the adults on board sailed the boat.

I was on watch at 0300 and the wind fell light just as we picked up the beam from Orfordness lighthouse. I checked that the disk brake, which stops the prop-shaft turning when we are under sail, was off, then started the engine. There was a slight smell of burning so I stopped the engine and made sure that the brake was definitely off, before re-starting the engine. Shortly afterwards, the skipper glanced below and saw a white glow through a chink in the floorboards! He yelled out

'Fire, Fire! Get lots of water, the brake disk and pads are white hot!'

I dashed to the galley and filled a basin with water, which I poured on the now exposed shaft brake. Meanwhile, Ian got the deck hose going and Jack, Nigel and Chris got the crew on deck. When the water hit the hot brake disk, the cabin filled instantly with steam so dense that nothing could be seen.

Now that the situation was under control, we took stock. The shaft brake had slipped into the 'on' position although the control wheel showed it as 'off'. We would have it fixed on our return to Ipswich. Despite our fire drill at the start of the cruise not one of the crew had brought a lifejacket with them when they had come on deck. We had spare ones on deck beside the life rafts, but it was quite a salutary lesson on how quickly an emergency could arise and how important fire drills were.

At break of day we had a pleasant sail up the Orwell to Pin Mill where we stopped to clean up the boat, then went on to our mooring at Ipswich, for debriefing and dispersal.

The teacher in charge of the Harrogate girls came on board and asked Alan how the girls had fared on the cruise. He said that he had been disappointed by their performance and he was not prepared to sign their assessment forms for the Duke of Edinburgh's Award. He had been more impressed with the two local crew youngsters who had taken the cruise more seriously.

This was the only occasion on an OYC voyage when I too felt I had been let down by crew members. Most of them rose to the challenge and were exhilarated by their experience.

In the course of our voyage I had recognised many of the sandbanks, buoys and navigational marks mentioned in Ransome's book. When I got home, I searched out my copy, and now with more insight, re-read it with great enjoyment.

Vere Harbour

Chapter 17 – Bound for the Great Barrier Reef

As we laboured to carry a sixteen-stone casualty up a steep river bank on a trestle table borrowed from the Dalesbridge Outdoor Centre, a concerned motorist stopped.

'Can we be of any help?' he asked.

'No thanks!' I called out as I struggled to keep my footing in slushy melting snow, 'It's an exercise!' One demanding exercise of many, on that assessment and training weekend at Settle in West Yorkshire. We were all aspirants to take part in the Ocean Youth Club's World Voyage.

That weekend about a hundred young people aged sixteen to twenty-four and adult voluntary mates like myself, had applied to sail on one or more legs of the Ocean Youth Club's eighteen-month world voyage involving more than 300 people on two sixty-nine-foot steel yachts, *James Cook* and *John Laing*.

A week or so later I was offered a place as a second mate on *John Laing* on Leg Seven from Sydney to Darwin, in July-August 1996. The sea staff on board would comprise a skipper, first mate, three second mates, and a bosun. The crew would be twelve young people.

To accept the offer, I would have to take early retirement. I had become headmaster of Barrhead High School in 1973 and rector of Eastwood High School at Newton Mearns in 1977. I had planned to retire at sixty but now left my post eighteen months early at the age of fifty-eight to sail in Australia. I had a year to prepare for my adventure.

I took the Long-range Radio Officer's Certificate course at Glasgow College of Nautical Studies. My successful completion of the course qualified me to operate the boat's HF radio and its satellite communications system which would enable us to report its position daily to OYC head office in Gosport.

The Ocean Youth Club also arranged for me to join another assessment and training group for a day at the Royal Navy's Damage Repair Instructional and Sea Survival Training Units at HMS *Excellent* at Portsmouth in October 1995.

After very basic training, we were formed into damage control teams for an exercise in a simulator. This was a full-size mock-up of three decks of a frigate. With the whole structure rocking to simulate a ship in a seaway, we coped for forty minutes with a simulated Exocet Missile attack; the sudden inflow of water came up to our waists in seconds. We blocked up holes in the hull, and pumped out water under the watchful guidance of instructor petty officers.

I would never forget this exciting experience and hoped we would not have to put any of it into practice on the voyage, but collision with floating objects capable of holing a boat was a real hazard at sea, ranging from escaped cargo containers to sleeping whales.

The day course concluded with sea survival training in a salt-water lake. After donning survival suits, we jumped into the water from a high tower, swam on our backs to a life raft, climbed in with great difficulty, prepared for a lengthy stay before rescue, and learned how to cope with hypothermia.

Leg One of the World Voyage left on 14 December 1995

from Southampton to the Canaries and was very demanding with eighteen days of beating south into gale force winds. A life raft disappeared in the high seas overnight and had to be replaced at Corunna. A seventeen-year-old crew member lost two stones on this three-week leg. Mouldy clothes were a further frustration. By complete contrast, Leg Two from the Canaries to Antigua was a delight. Swimming in mid-Atlantic, dolphins, whales and incredible sunrises and sunsets made the trip memorable. The two yachts had a great welcome at English Harbour, Antigua. Leg Three from Antigua to Panama went well, visiting St. Maarten, Anguilla, and the British Virgin Islands. There were some delays due to maintenance at Panama, then the yachts made the long Leg Four passage to Tahiti arriving on Monday 13 May 1996. After a successful Leg Five voyage to Auckland, the boats changed crews for Leg Six to Sydney. They had variable winds on passage, and a severe gale in the Tasman Sea.

I was now ready to join *John Laing* at Sydney for Leg Seven from Sydney to Darwin. I flew from London, via Vancouver and Honolulu. I had chosen to travel westwards with journey stops, to avoid jet lag.

On arrival at Sydney on Wednesday 17 July I joined the yachts which were moored at the National Maritime Museum at Darling Harbour. I met the skipper of *John Laing*, Chris Dobson, his first mate Andy Royal, and the skipper of *James Cook*, Brian Eyres. The other second mates, bosuns and crews joined us the following day, arriving on board at 0700, and very tired after their flight from London.

The ship's company of *John Laing* comprised:
Skipper - Chris Dobson and his fiancée Liz

First mate - Andy Royal

Second mates - Heather Johnston, Ian Macpherson and Mark Underwood

Port watch - boys Antony, Mark, and Geoff, and girls Nic, Carrie and Pippa

Starboard watch - boys, Nick, James and C-J, and girls Polly, Lou and Cassie.

After cleaning the boat on Friday 19 July, we had a day off for sightseeing, which I spent at Manly with James, a keen surfer.

On Saturday 20 July we spent the morning on sail training then set off at 1530 for Brisbane in a rising south-west wind, making six knots under number two jib alone. We passed Sydney Bridge and the Opera House into the magnificent natural harbour, then past Manly and Sydney Heads into the Tasman Sea. It was a rough night and my first watch was 2000 to 2400. I had been relieved by Mark at midnight in a rising wind and was glad to turn in for a rest.

OYC ketch *John Laing (Photograph by OYT South)*

Chapter 18 – Into the tropics

'My first soaking!' exclaimed Mark Underwood, my fellow mate on *John Laing*, scrambling out of sodden clothes as he came off watch at 0400 on Sunday 21 July 1996.

I had been relieved by Mark at midnight in a rising wind; from the relative comfort of my wildly tossing bunk I could hear the wind as it rose to a south-westerly gale, and the concerned but controlled voices of Mark and our skipper Chris Dobson directing the crew on watch.

A double reef went into the mainsail, and a run down-wind enabled the number two jib to be dropped, but water coming over the bow soaked the foredeck crew to their waists in seconds. The staysail was raised in its place, then the boat was turned northwards once again. We had not expected this gale on our first night out from Sydney, but after all, it was winter sailing in Australia.

I had half expected to be called back on deck in the night to help, but I had not been needed. I blessed the civilised watch system set up by our first mate, Andy Royal, which kept the second mates fresh and ready for emergencies. Our three second mates worked one watch on and two watches off. It was harder for our young crew who worked one watch on and one watch off. From 0800-2000 we ran two six-hour watches, and during darkness from 2000 to 0800 we ran three four-hour watches. This gave automatic rotation and all three mates, Mark Underwood, Heather Johnston and myself, worked with both duty watches and so got to know all the crew.

The sea was lumpy. The adverse East Australian Current did not help, but by mid-afternoon on Sunday 21 July the wind had dropped, and we had caught up with our sister-ship *James Cook*. Each acting as the other's safety boat, we kept within ten miles of each other and were in radio contact every two hours. Keeping together was not easy, as *John Laing* was the faster yacht and sometimes had to reduce sail or reef to let *James Cook* catch up.

As we approached Gold Coast, the surfing area of Queensland, the winds became light, it was noticeably warmer, and we had beautiful sunsets. The night sky was magnificent and we quickly identified the Southern Cross. Venus and Jupiter were prominent, the Milky Way was much brighter than in the Northern Hemisphere, and Orion could be seen upside down on the northern horizon.

We saw many meteors, some very spectacular as they burnt themselves out in the upper atmosphere. We watched one or two satellites passing across the dark sky. It took a little time to get used to looking northwards for the sun and to watch it cross the sky from right to left.

A beautiful sunrise on Tuesday 23 July was preceded by an indigo and red light on the horizon and a mirage image gave us a double sun for a few seconds at dawn.

Off Cape Byron, Australia's most easterly point, we sailed into a pod of black and white killer whales. About twenty whales sported around the two yachts. They broached, fluked (slapped their tails on the water), and leapt to right and left. Their prominent high dorsal fins were everywhere, and some blew close to the boats startling the crews.

It was a great welcome to Gold Coast, and on the morning of Wednesday 24 July we slipped over the bar (just, as we touched briefly) into berths at Southport Yacht Club, beside high-rise hotels and all the buzz of Surfers' Paradise. The yacht club made us very welcome and we appreciated the showers and laundry facilities.

The yacht club was quite formal; the waitresses in the restaurant wore epaulettes. Andy Methley, a mate on *James Cook*, was asked to change out of his immaculate white singlet with tasteful logo into something with a collar before he could be served a meal. Without a word, he left immediately and returned five minutes later, wearing a horrible red and white striped Patrick Thistle 2nd XI strip with a collar!

We were very sorry to lose a popular member of our crew here who had been continuously seasick since we left Sydney. After much thought he flew home from Brisbane. We nearly lost James the surfer who had difficulty paddling ashore after being carried out to sea on his hired surfboard. No wonder he fell asleep at the dining table that night.

Despite the well-developed resort area there were sea eagles everywhere, and an attractive maze of shallow waterways led north towards Fraser Island. They were too shallow for us to use however, and on Thursday 25 July we sailed out to sea bound for the Whitsunday Islands. The forecast of another gale made us put into Mooloolaba the next day, where their yacht club gave us hospitality and James bought a bargain surfboard, which soon occupied the vacant berth.

No gale materialised, so we set off again on Saturday 27 July straight into a near-gale with heavy hailstones. I came on watch at midnight and like several others was surprised to be suddenly seasick as we motored into heavy seas. I was tired and ready to go below at the end of my watch at 0400.

During the morning we got close to the southern entrance to the Great Sandy Strait between Fraser Island and the mainland shore, but a line of white breakers on the bar made us think again. A mile off the broken water we turned away to go outside Fraser Island and its Seventy-five Mile Beach.

The seas moderated and we had good reaching westerly winds as we sped north past the Bunker Group of islands. Dolphins appeared many times and looked spectacular in the early morning light, swimming within the wave crests to windward. Our whale book identified them as pantropic spotted dolphins

At 1800 on Monday 29 July, Chris announced that we were now just within the southern extremity of the Great Barrier Reef, and at 2044 we crossed the tropic of Capricorn.

Volleyball on Hamilton Island

Ian at the helm, in Gulf of Carpentaria, Australia

Chapter 19 – The Whitsundays and Cairns

At sunrise on Tuesday 30 July, Heather saw a great whale leap clean out of the water, outlined against the sun's rising disc. Soon afterwards we saw large bottlenose dolphins.

In the late afternoon the call of 'Whale!' brought us all on deck to have a very good sighting of a humpbacked whale. It waved its huge tail at us before diving, and re-emerged ten minutes later with a great 'Whoosh!' of fishy breath right alongside the yacht.

It was exhilarating at night, with bright moonlight overhead, to sail fast in near gale west-south-west winds with number three jib and double reefed main up, keeping a careful eye on *James Cook*. At one stage we reached eight and a half knots. (We averaged 5.2 knots over the whole voyage).

We sailed up the Northumberland Passage outside a string of islands which are a nature reserve. By late afternoon on Wednesday 31 July we had reached the first of the Cumberland Islands, usually known as the Whitsundays named after the most prominent of these hilly wooded islands. As dusk fell, we sailed up the Cumberland Channel past St. Bees Island towards Hamilton Island. We had to wait until dawn for the tide to rise, before we could enter Hamilton Harbour.

Hamilton was a highly developed private resort island with an airport and attractive hotels. We refuelled and had a twenty-four-hour break. Highlights there were showers, snorkelling, and a volleyball match on the beach against Cook's crew.

At dusk, hundreds of huge flying foxes (fruit bats) with a metre wingspan wheeled above their roost beside the marina before flying off in vast flocks to their feeding grounds. In the evening we met a former OYC Australia skipper, Jonathon, who showed us over a luxurious yacht which he now skippered, owned by an Australian businessman originally from Falkirk in Scotland.

On the way back to the boat at midnight we saw a surreal scene illuminated by floodlights behind a baker's shop on the waterfront. ET-like little wallabies were sitting quietly, eating the day's leftover buns.

At 0600 on Friday 2nd August we sailed beyond neighbouring Whitsunday Island to Hook Island for a day's swimming and snorkelling. The highly coloured fish were fascinating. As a steady current carried the swimmers down the side of Hook Island, we were glad to have our Avon safety boat to pick us up and take us back to the beach. Two boys with coral cuts had to be treated with antiseptic powder as coral infections in the tropics could be nasty.

In the evening we went on our way, making for Cairns. I was the duty mate responsible that day for meals being on time, and supervised the roasting of three shoulders of lamb, a legacy in our deep freeze from New Zealand. A gift of lamb had fed the previous Leg Six crew for weeks.

We ate very well on the trip, with a good selection of frozen meat and plenty of fruit and vegetables topped up at our ports of call. We also baked bread, and Andy even received a tentative proposal of marriage on the strength of his proficiency in baking scones and cakes.

The weather was now very hot and with calm seas due to the reef's shelter we were able to practise taking sextant shots of the sun at mid-day. As we plotted our hourly positions with our GPS, our sextants were a back-up.

Shipping now became busy as we approached Cairns and a sharp lookout was essential as we dodged tankers, container vessels and prawn boats off Townsville and Magnetic Island. We reached Cairns at 2130 on Sunday 4 August, following the five-metre depth line along the coast with our echo-sounder until we reached the marked channel leading into Cairns. Above the casino, three searchlight beams played constantly in the night sky.

I spent a marvellous day on Green Island, a coral atoll near Cairns, which I visited on a diving excursion by motor catamaran. The other participants were a group of Japanese scuba divers, who dived on the deep outer edge of the coral reef. I snorkelled on the shallow island side of the coral reef. I swam over beautiful pink, blue, and yellow corals, branched, brain-shaped or cup-shaped, amongst shoals of highly coloured fish. I even found a giant clam with purple mantle and two black waving vents. In the distance, off the steep outer edge of the reef, large fish wheeled and pursued smaller fish.

My last day at Cairns was spent on the Atherton Tablelands to the south of the city. Roger, a mate on *James Cook*, C-J and I, hired a car for the day and drove past sugarcane fields, banana plantations and a mango farm. We had a swim and picnic lunch at Josephine Falls, and stopped at Millaa Millaa Falls. We drove up to the tablelands and visited Lake Eacham, a crater lake where we had another swim and saw pelicans, fish and small turtles. A brief stop at Lake Barradine preceded our descent of the escarpment by a twisting road down to the plain.

We left for Darwin at 2130 on 6 August on a ten-day non-stop voyage. We motored in light wind. The crew were tired. Some had gone diving on the Great Barrier Reef, and James the surfer had gone on a bungee jump, landing head first in a pool of water. He said it had been a wonderful experience, well worth the forty-five pounds it had cost.

I was on watch on Wednesday 7 August from 0400-0800, so I saw daybreak as we passed the spot where Captain Cook had had his problems, as indicated by the names he gave to Cape Tribulation, Mount Sorrow and Mount Misery. He also named the happier Mount Halcyon, and Cooktown is where he careened *Endeavour* for repairs after she had grounded on Endeavour Reef. Once past Endeavour Reef and Cooktown we poled out the number one jib and sailed goose-winged with jib and mainsail. In the late evening we passed the Howick Group of Islands in an east-south-east fresh breeze. Could we now be in the south-east trade winds?

Return of shore party at Hook Island

Chapter 20 – Rounding Cape York

I was on watch from 0800-1400 on Thursday 8 August, when we crossed Princess Charlotte Bay. The day had begun with a light shower; all day it was hot and humid. By 1130 the temperature was twenty-seven degrees C. We changed sail to the red, white, and yellow cruising chute. Off to starboard we could see *James Cook* raising her mizzen staysail as well as her blue cruising chute to stay on station.

When we passed the Flinders Islands, the edge of the Great Barrier Reef was only six miles offshore, and there was an increase in shipping. We passed prawn boats anchored off Eden Reef. These fishermen worked at night and slept by day.

It was Carrie's eighteenth birthday. We decorated the saloon, baked a chocolate sponge birthday cake and gave her the day's chart, which we had all signed, as a present. At lunchtime the extrovert Geoff delivered a stripper-gram to her from her shipmates. He began his delivery in heavy OYC oilskins and ended up in fetching lingerie!

We were now making fast progress north in the south-east trade wind helped by a north-going current. It was a busy night. Large oil tankers passed us in both directions and we could see another yacht coming up behind us, the only yacht we saw north of Cairns. Chris was up most of the night taking half-hourly radar fixes in the narrow shipping channel. He asked duty mates to rouse him if any vessel approached within two miles of us.

The OYC yachts rounded Cape York at 0100 on Saturday 10 August. We slipped through the three-quarter-mile gap between Meddler Island to the north and Possession Island to the south, to enter Endeavour Strait. Only shallow draft vessels use Endeavour Strait. Captain Cook had claimed possession of Australia by Britain on this island to port. As we passed into the Gulf of Carpentaria there was a depth of only six point three metres under us.

The south-east trade wind now piped up, and we rolled our way westwards in rain squalls and strong winds. For three days we sailed without sighting another vessel. On Sunday 11 August, *John Laing* again got ahead of *James Cook*, so we dropped the main and mizzen, proceeded under number two jib only, and we deliberately overtightened the jib sheet. This got our speed down to three and a half knots and at last *James Cook* appeared on the horizon at 1400.

We had a hilarious Blind Date Session over the VHF radio with *James Cook*'s crew. A girl from *Cook* chose one of our boys from a choice of three for a date in Darwin.

As we rolled along in a steady swell from the south, we saw some movement in the sea ahead, and suddenly realised that we were watching flying fishes. Soon afterwards we passed black dolphins and two turtles. By the late afternoon of Monday 12 August we were passing Cape Jessel on the islands to the north-east of Arnhem Land.

Our westward progress was marked by a brilliant display of shooting stars in the early morning of Tuesday 13 August. We were still on Sydney time, which was getting out of step with local time. As we sailed westward, sunrise was now around 0700 rather than 0630.

On the morning of Wednesday 14 August, a small red and white twin-engine customs plane flew low over us. What was it looking for?

We gybed to sail north of New Year Island; we could see its lighthouse gleaming in the sun.

At 1600 we held a kangaroo court over the VHF radio with *James Cook's* crew. A girl on *Cook* was accused of stealing a pair of a boy's underpants. Our jury found her not guilty, but framed!

There was a puzzling incident in the night on Thursday 15 August at 0400, eight miles off Wanry Point on the Cobourg Peninsula. We were watching *James Cook's* echo on the radar, and spotted a strong second echo to the west of Cook.

The vessel responsible showed no navigational lights, and did not respond to our VHF radio inquiry. *James Cook* moved closer, within two hundred metres of the ship, and Brian shone its bright Aldis lamp in its direction. The vessel was not sighted and we watched it move off rapidly on our radar screen.

Was this what yesterday's spotter plane had been looking for? We thought that the mystery ship might have been a smuggler of drugs or people from Indonesia into Australia. We reported the ship to Darwin Radio.

We arrived in Darwin at 0800 on Friday 16 August and locked into Fishermen's Wharf Basin. After breakfast, a thorough clean-up of *John Laing* continued till 1300. The sweat poured of us in thirty degrees C, and we relished the hot showers - our first for ten days - at the shore end of the wharf.

When we had berthed at Cairns on our way north, we could hear the sound of salt-water crocodiles splashing in the harbour as we lay in our bunks at night. There was a crocodile farm just outside Darwin and I decided to visit it to learn more about these intriguing creatures. There we saw small freshwater crocodiles, which are not dangerous, being reared for their attractive patterned leather, and huge salt-water crocodiles who had been captured and brought here when they had become man-eating menaces in their home areas.

These crocodile prisoners were kept in a large pond. They were fed regularly on chicken carcases. To signal mealtime their keeper thumped a chicken carcase on the bank and immediately, large numbers of crocodiles began to swim purposefully towards him. He held out a chicken on the end of a pole to the first crocodile. It leapt out of the water on to the bank at an incredible speed and snatched the chicken before retreating back into the water. I was glad to be on the opposite side of the fence enclosing the lagoon.

The following morning there was a crew change. Half of our crew flew back to London, and the others went to Cairns or Brisbane.

When I left the yacht at Darwin, I visited the Kakadu National Park on a minibus camping trip, organised by Trailfinders. There we saw a host of saltwater crocodiles on the banks of Yellow Waters, a branch of the South Alligator River.

A flat-bottomed boat with an outboard motor took us close by large crocodiles sunning themselves on the river-bank. It looked an idyllic scene. Wild horses (brumbies) browsed in the water-meadows and tropical birds including egrets, storks and waterfowl were abundant, but the river was dominated by the crocodiles.

We saw more at the East Alligator River marking the edge of Arnhemland, near a shallow ford. We were horrified to see a four-wheel vehicle drive across from Arnhemland preceded by a girl who waded across. She was lucky to make it with crocodiles so near. Other people earlier in the year had not.

Whales and crocodiles are amazing creatures, and I had been so lucky to have seen them in their natural habitats.

Our cruise had been a marvellous adventure. We had made it! We had sailed 2,627 miles from Sydney to Darwin, and I felt proud at the age of fifty-nine to have been an OYC mate on Leg Seven of the Ocean Youth Club World Voyage.

 OCEAN YOUTH CLUB
OYC

Ocean Youth Club
World Voyage 1995 - 1997

This is to certify that
Ian Macpherson
was a staff member on the yacht
John Laing

On Leg Seven the yachts made passage from Sydney, inside the Great Barrier Reef, to Darwin. En route they stopped at Southport, Mooloolaba, Hamilton Island, Hook Island, and Cairns.

On the World Voyage the sea staff instruct a group of 16-24 year olds in how to maintain and operate a 70ft yacht. Staff must motivate the group to work in an unfamiliar environment, often in adverse conditions.

Leg Seven - Sydney to Darwin
16 Jul 96 - 18 Aug 96
Days on board - 32
Distance sailed - 2,627 nm
Maximum wind strength - F8

Jeremy Black

Admiral Sir Jeremy Black GBE KCB DSO
Chairman World Voyage Steering Committee

OYC World Voyage Certificate

Chapter 21 – *Rum Runner*

I had always wanted to own my own yacht, and when I returned from Australia in 1996 I set about looking for a suitable second-hand vessel. My friend Reay Mackay told me of a yacht that had just come on to the market at Rhu Marina near Helensburgh. The owner and his wife had been keen sailors and on his wife's death he had decided to sell the yacht.

The boat was a classic Nicholson 35 called *Rum Runner*, a heavily built boat with a deep keel, she was ideal for cruising the west coast of Scotland. She was twenty-three years old with a Perkins diesel engine but in very good condition. Reay gave her a once-over, tested the diesel engine which had a hydraulic drive, and gave her the thumbs up. I had her surveyed, made an offer which was accepted in November 1996, and spent the winter getting her ready at Rhu Marina for the 1997 sailing season.

An article appeared in Yachting Monthly in February 1997 about a cruise the previous owners had made in the yacht in 1995 to the Monach Islands to the west of South Uist.

I based *Rum Runner* at Largs Marina and she competed in the 1997 Barrhead Bell Trophy Race off Largs on 9th May 1997; she took line honours but was third on handicap.

Later that month, I took *Rum Runner* through the Crinan Canal to visit the Garvellachs, a group of small islands in the Firth of Lorne west of Luing. My crew were my sister Morag and her partner Guy, who were visiting us from Australia, and my brother Donald.

We sailed from Largs to Tarbert on Loch Fyne, and the following morning entered the Crinan Canal at Lochgilphead. We enjoyed operating the locks and motored leisurely through the verdant countryside. In the distance we could see the green mound of the ancient fortress of Dunadd, seat of the Kings of Dalriada in the Dark Ages. We tied up at a landing stage near the Crinan basin for an overnight stop and locked out into the Sound of Jura in the morning.

Once past the entrance to the Gulf of Corryveckan, we had a hard beat up the Sound of Luing, then sailed westwards to the Garvellachs or Isles of the Sea. We anchored in a narrow sheltered bay on Eileach an Naoimh and rowed ashore in our rubber dinghy.

This island had a monastery founded by St. Brendan in 542 A.D., which was destroyed in later centuries by the Vikings. It was said to have been a favourite place for contemplation by St. Columba, and his mother may have been buried here where there is a gravestone marked with a cross.

There are monastery ruins and monks' beehive cells near the landing place, and I sensed a distinct unsettling atmosphere about these quiet ancient buildings. I was not surprised to hear that the island was reputed to be haunted.

From the Garvellachs we had a fast sail to the Cuan Sound at the north end of Luing. We timed our passage through the sound to catch a favourable tidal stream, as the tide runs very fast in the narrow sound. We emerged into Seil Sound, and sailed into Loch Melfort. We spent the night on pontoons at the holiday resort at the head of the loch, and enjoyed an excellent dinner at the restaurant.

We left Loch Melfort the next morning and anchored off

Arduaine Garden at the entrance to the loch. The row ashore to visit the garden was well worthwhile, as like the gardens at Inverewe, it contained many exotic plants. Now we sailed south, taking advantage of a push from the tide to enter Loch Craignish, and stopped overnight at the moorings at Ardfern.

On our return passage through the Crinan Canal we again stopped overnight at a landing stage. This time we were near one of the lock gates on a middle stretch of the canal. I went for an evening walk before dinner and looked over the lock gate. The canal beyond it was completely dry! It had been drained for maintenance work, but a canal worker assured me that the empty stretch of canal would be full of water again in the morning.

We exited the canal at Ardrishaig in the morning, and sailed south down Loch Fyne, through the Kyles of Bute and back to Largs Marina. It had been an enjoyable trip in sunny weather made memorable by the beautiful scenery and interesting places we had visited.

During the sailing season from March to October, I spent most weekends on *Rum Runner* in the Firth of Clyde, round Arran, through the spectacular Kyles of Bute, or on Loch Fyne around Tarbert. My regular crew were Tim West, Jim Strong and Douglas Walker.

I now considered a cruise to Ireland's Donegal coast and did my research for the trip during the winter of 1997-98. I looked at pilot books, charts and almanacs, and scoured yachting magazines for accounts of cruises on the west coast of Ireland. I chose our route and anchorages carefully, and I looked for alternatives should wind and weather cause difficulties.

Rotary Race Barrhead Bell winners 2000
Left to right, Iain Provan, Douglas Walker, Ian, and Ed Crangle

Rum Runner at Kyles of Bute *(Photograph by Ross Ritchie)*

Chapter 22 – Donegal?

We set off in my yacht *Rum Runner* from Largs bound for Donegal on Saturday 25 July 1998. There were four of us on this cruise. Alastair my first mate had qualified as a yacht designer but now worked in I.T. He and I were both experienced sailors. Tim and Douglas were both professional engineers. Tim and Douglas had sailed with me frequently and had helped me with winter boat maintenance. Douglas was relatively new to sailing.

Our crossing to Lamlash behind Holy Isle on Arran in bright sunny weather was straightforward. We had the usual tussle at Lamlash with the anchor as holding there is poor, but eventually, at the third attempt, the anchor dug in and we stayed there overnight.

There was exceptionally heavy rain as we left Lamlash in the morning and visibility was almost zero, but the rain stopped as we neared the isle of Pladda off Kildonan, and suddenly we could see its lighthouse in the morning sun. Three and a half hours later we reached Campbeltown on the Kintyre Peninsula.

We left Campbeltown for Ireland at 1000 on Monday 27 July. Once past Sanda island, we got a good fix at 1400 for our point of departure off the Mull of Kintyre. Careful navigation was required as the tide was setting us north. We made for Rathlin island off the Antrim coast. Taking care in the fast tidal streams around Rathlin, we reached Ballycastle at 1800, where we tied up at its little marina.

George Kemp, assistant to Marconi the radio pioneer sent Morse radio signals from Ballycastle to Rathlin lighthouse in 1896. This then enabled Lloyd's of London to get early shipping news of vessels passing Rathlin lighthouse.

The next day we caught the west-going tide to help us to sail up Rathlin Sound, then sailed past Benbane Head, the Giant's Causeway and Portrush on our way to Colraine in County Londonderry. Colraine lay four miles up a buoyed channel on the River Bann, whose mouth was marked by two training walls, which help to keep its entrance channel clear. We tied up at 1410 on pontoons at Colraine Marina, and were made very welcome at the Colraine Yacht Club.

Our next destination would be Lough Swilly in Donegal in the Irish Republic. The weather forecast on Wednesday 29 July gave a west-north-west moderate breeze, backing west in the afternoon. We would be beating round Malin Head. We left Colraine at 1110 and once clear of the river mouth I called the coastguard on VHF radio to tell them our destination and gave our estimated time of arrival at Lough Swilly. They acknowledged, and wished us good sailing. A minute later we were listening to another message on VHF calling channel sixteen.

'*Rum Runner, Rum Runner* this is Salutay!' I acknowledged, and changed channels.

'*Rum Runner* this is Salutay,' said the steady, pleasant Irish voice.

'We overheard your call to Belfast Coastguard giving your ETA at Loch Swilly. We have just rounded Malin Head and there are heavy seas here. Now, I don't know if your crew are men of resolution and determination, or how big your boat is, but we are a seventy-foot diving boat and my men don't like the seas here one bit! If I were you, I would consider carefully if you *really* want to round Malin Head today.'

I thanked Salutay's skipper for his helpful information and we considered the situation. We decided it would be prudent to wait another day at Colraine.

I turned Rum Runner away from Inishowen Head, back towards the two training walls at Barmouth the river entrance.

We dropped the sails, and as I took the helm under engine a sudden rain squall cut across our bows hiding the river entrance. I was on the point of turning out to sea again until visibility improved, when the squall passed and Alastair called out that we were now off the line of the leading marks. I brought *Rum Runner* on to the transit line, and we surfed into the river mouth. We enjoyed the pastoral peace and quiet of the river passage back to Colraine.

Next morning, we set off again. There had been heavy rain in the night and the river was in spate. The wind was now north-north-west and blowing straight into the river mouth. Between the training walls three huge standing waves had gleaming brown water surging over them.

Rum Runner crested the first wave and ploughed into the back of the second wave. A surge of water sluiced over the deck into the cockpit and we were up to our knees in water. I increased engine revs and we progressed out to sea, which was quite rough in the cross-tide flooding toward Lough Foyle. So rough, that in raising the mainsail, its halyard rope jammed around the radar reflector on the front of the mast. There was nothing for it but to get into a quiet harbour to clear the rope. I did not fancy returning to the Bann so we made for Portrush.

We surfed on big waves to the harbour entrance in the onshore wind, then turned sharply to port to get into the shelter of the harbour wall.

Once the boat was tied up and the halyard had been cleared, we could relax after our fraught morning. We chatted to a live-aboard yachtsman whose motor yacht lay next to us. He was waiting for the seas to moderate before taking his boat up to Colraine. He said that the previous week two yachts had come to grief entering the River Bann. One had piled up on the beach on one side of the river mouth and the other had foundered on the rocks on the other side.

The northwest wind seemed settled for the next day or so, and we now abandoned our plan to sail to Donegal as we would be on an exposed coast. However, the wind was fair for Islay and we had the appropriate charts, so the next day we set off for Port Ellen on Islay.

It was a cracking beat for six hours in bright sunny weather in a north-west fresh breeze. The Mull of Oa had been visible from Portrush and we made a good landfall at Port Ellen. As we approached the harbour we prepared to lower the sails and I switched on the engine. Nothing happened!

Although we were tired, the sun was shining, which lifted our spirits, and we set about getting the boat safely anchored or moored under sail. I remembered that there were visitors' moorings in the bay, so we could pick one up. First, we doubled reefed the sails to reduce speed, then we tacked towards the lighthouse where we swung round to starboard on to a broad reach which took us a towards the row of mooring buoys. We kept our speed down further by furling the genoa completely and over-tightening the double-reefed mainsail. Aiming for the middle buoy, we rounded up into the wind and caught it at the first attempt. We dropped the mainsail and relaxed at last.

Rum Runner at Colraine Marina

Chapter 23 – The Inner Hebrides

It was Friday 31 July 1998. We lay on our mooring at Port Ellen with a dead engine. A test meter placed across the battery terminals gave a lowish reading. I now radioed the coastguard to announce our safe arrival at Port Ellen. I advised them that we had engine trouble, most likely due to a low battery. They said they would try to get some help to us and within half an hour David Stephenson, skipper of the fishing boat *Pioneer* from Port Ellen arrived with the local voluntary coastguard Peter Campbell on board.

They lent us a fully charged battery which we fitted, but still could not start the engine. Another local man, Ian Newman arrived in an Islay Diving Centre boat. He thought that our starter solenoid switch was faulty and tried to start the engine by short circuiting the solenoid switch with two large crossed screwdrivers with insulated handles. There was a big bang, sparks flew, and the engine started with a roar. The fishermen cheered!

We motored over to the pier, and tied up. The engine was shut down and we refitted our own batteries. Tim started the engine using the same trick as before, which I later found described in Nigel Calder's book *Repairs at Sea*.

I was relieved that he did not electrocute himself. We charged the batteries for a couple of hours and decided to sort out the starter switch in the morning. That evening we enjoyed a delicious Ulster leg of lamb, which I had bought in Portrush.

I went ashore in the morning in search of a garage engineer who might be able to fix our starter solenoid problem. I had no success, and returned to the boat somewhat despondent, where I found the crew wreathed in smiles. Alastair had found a loose wire hidden behind the solenoid starter switch. When the wire was reconnected, the engine started at the first turn of the key. There were grins all round and the sun shone!

We did some shopping at Port Ellen, a quiet attractive little port, which suddenly came to life with the arrival of the Caledonian MacBrayne ferry from Kennacraig on the Kintyre Peninsula.

The crew of *Pioneer* retrieved their battery but refused any payment for their services. We were offered mackerel, which we accepted gratefully and responded with some cans of beer for our friends. We had appreciated their assistance and the local tradition of mutual help impressed us.

Our next stop was Craighouse on Jura. We had left Port Ellen in a moderate north-north-west wind, which gradually diminished and backed into the west. By 1720 we were becalmed, and another hour's motoring got us to Craighouse where we anchored.

The next morning, we left at 0800 to catch the north-going tidal stream up the Sound of Islay. Winds were light as we tacked into the sound, and died away by 0900. We motored the rest of the way to Scalasaig on Colonsay, which I had last visited in July 1986 on *Goodbye Girl*. We tied up at the pier at 1315 and were greeted by a friendly seal who was waiting for a fishing boat to arrive. We had received a gale 'soon' warning mid-morning, so could expect strong winds in the evening.

In the afternoon we walked to the southern end of Colonsay to visit the tidal island of Ornsay, which has ruins of an ancient priory, but by the time we reached the beach opposite Ornsay the tide had risen and we were unable to cross over.

We left Colonsay at noon on Monday 3 August bound for the island of Gigha with a north-west moderate breeze behind us. As the wind was rising, we put a reef in the mainsail. By the time we passed the lighthouse at McArthur's Head it was blowing north-west near gale straight out of the Sound of Islay, and the sea was getting very rough.

I hove-to, to put a second reef in the main in more comfort. Once *Rum Runner* was pointing into the wind with a backed genoa, and the helm lashed down to keep her there, the change in her motion was very marked. Now the waves rolled under her and shot off to leeward while she moved up and down and under control.

I clipped my safety harness line to the steel cable safety lines, which ran from bow to cockpit on either side of the mast, and moved forward on the high side of the boat to help with the reefing. I was suddenly aware that Douglas had not hooked his safety harness line to the safety cable. I yelled at him to hook on, and was relieved to see him do so without mishap. Once reefed, we all returned safely to the cockpit, I unfastened the lashing on the wheel, and turned the boat downwind. She shot off towards Cara, the small island at the south end of Gigha, the wind now gusting at thirty knots. At 1830 we tied up to a visitor's mooring beside the Gigha Hotel at Ardminish.

I had planned our passage round the Mull of Kintyre on Tuesday 4 August. If we left Gigha at 1000 we should catch the east-going tidal stream round the Mull around 1330.

We gave it a go for two hours, but with a west-south-west wind gusting at twenty-five to thirty knots and heavy seas, we thought it best to return to Gigha and wait for more favourable weather.

The following day we left Gigha at 1025 in a light south-west wind. At 1100 we received another gale warning – south-west F 8 'soon'. At 1200 the wind dropped to light airs from the south-west, so we dropped the genoa and motored for forty minutes till the wind returned, a west-south-west moderate breeze. By 1400 Machrihanish was abeam, and the Mull of Kintyre Lighthouse was sited. On the rocks at the Mull there was a colony of about a hundred large seals.

We cleared the Mull at 1500 with help from the engine to counter the adverse tide. A light west wind now took us to Sanda Sound and, as the wind died away, we motored to Campbeltown, which we reached at 1915.

On Thursday 6 August we set of for Tarbert on Loch Fyne. We made good progress up Kilbrannan Sound in a west wind with showery weather but did not see much of Arran till we reached Lochranza.

Off Skipness Point we came across porpoises, and a large basking shark, almost as long as *Rum Runner*, languidly swimming north with its dorsal and tail fins above the surface undulating slowly to and fro. Its huge open mouth would have been gathering the rich plankton, which attracts them here each summer.

Once into Loch Fyne the wind increased, so we put reefs into the main and genoa at 1500. Ten minutes later we were hit by a vicious squall which screwed us up to windward. We hastily put a second reef into the sails. We reached Tarbert at 1630.

On Friday there was little wind, so we motored up Loch Fyne exploring it as far as Otter Ferry where we tied up to a mooring buoy for lunch. Returning to Tarbert in the afternoon the weather got increasingly wet and torrential rain confined us to the yacht that evening. We enjoyed rainbow trout for dinner.

On the last day of our cruise we returned to Largs via the Kyles of Bute. It was a pleasant sunny day with variable light winds. Off Tighnabruaich we met some friends, OYC mates on a training cruise on *Cherry Ripe*, being skippered by Ross Ritchie. The wind returned off Toward Point at 1510 giving us a good sail to Largs Marina in a fresh southerly wind. We berthed at 1700, having logged 416 miles on our cruise.

I enjoyed sailing *Rum Runner*, but the annual expenses of running her were considerable, and maintenance work took up a lot of my time. Marina costs for services all added up. These included berthing, winter storage, lifting the boat in and out of the water, and lifting the mast out for servicing, then putting it back in the boat at the start of the sailing season.

I did my own engine maintenance, serviced all the valves in the hull, and cleaned and antifouled the hull with help from Tim, Jim, and Douglas, but the life raft needed annual servicing, and I had to replace expensive emergency flares within their use-by dates. Varnishing the woodwork on deck at the start of each sailing season also took some time. Fortunately, I had a good wardrobe of sails, but replacing any of them would have been very expensive.

All this expenditure of money and time could only be justified if all our spare time and all our holidays were spent on *Rum Runner*, and crucially only with the enthusiastic support of Gill. Unfortunately, she did not like sailing.

After three sailing seasons, I sold Rum Runner in May 2000, and reverted to my previous practice of chartering yachts for limited periods.

Divers at Port Ellen

Good catch at Port Ellen

Chapter 24 – *Alba Venturer*

In 1997 I became the Ocean Youth Club's Scottish Area Governor. One of my responsibilities was finding a replacement for *Taikoo*, now 24 years old, as she was showing signs of her age and becoming more and more expensive to maintain.

We would apply to the Scottish Lottery Sports Fund for a grant of half the cost of replacing her. The other half would have to be raised ourselves. I discussed with the voluntary mates, how we might do this. We publicised our need for sponsorship and hoped that banks, industrial firms and others might be willing to help. Our bid for a grant was submitted to the Scottish National Sports Council, which was adjudicating bids.

In September 1997, I received a phone call from businessman Lionel Mills, better known as Curly Mills, the yachtsman who organised the Scottish Islands Peaks Race each year. *Taikoo* had often taken part in this race with teams of sailors and hill runners, so we had met Curly from time to time.

'I hear you are looking for funds to replace *Taikoo*,' said Curly. 'I'd like to help. My daughter sailed on *Taikoo* fifteen years ago and I know how much young people gain from the experience.'

I expressed my delight at his interest and told him of our Mainstay Business Association, which gave businesses which contributed to our funds various benefits, depending on the size of their donations.

'Oh,' he said, 'I don't want to contribute to part of the boat. I am interested in the whole boat!'

'Well,' I said, 'do you realise that we are talking about £800,000 for a seventy-foot Oyster yacht?'

'Is that what it would cost?' said Curly.

'How much would you want to contribute?' I cautiously ventured.

'As much as it takes!' he said. 'You see, I made a lot of money when I sold off my heating and ventilating business and I don't want the tax man to get it when I pop off, so I'd like to give it to the Ocean Youth Club for the new boat.'

I explained that we were submitting a Lottery bid for half the cost of a new boat, £400,000, and Curly agreed to send us this amount immediately.

We made the grant application to the Scottish Sports Council in November 1997. I attended a meeting of all the current applicants at the Scottish Sports Council in Edinburgh, where the application procedure was explained to us. No dialogue on our bids was permitted. In March 1998 we heard that our bid had been rejected. They would not consider a request for replacement of equipment or premises but would have considered a request for an additional boat to *Taikoo* more favourably.

When Curly heard the news he promptly gave the OYC another £400,000, so due to his generosity, which we very much appreciated, we could now go ahead with building the yacht. It was to be called *Alba Venturer* after Curly's firm Alba Diagnostics, which was a world leader in the diagnosis of car faults.

The yacht was to be a seventy-foot Oyster ketch with a production hull form, but with deck and interior designed by the Ocean Youth Trust (the OYC had by now been renamed). I chaired the Scottish Boat Committee, which planned the deck and interior layout and had oversight of its building.

A great deal of equipment was required for its fitting out and the Scottish Area manager Barry Fisher launched a successful appeal for donations for its purchase from industry, banks, charities and individuals. Nearly £100,000 was raised.

The OYT arranged regular visits to the boat to check on progress, but my first chance to see her was on 17 February 1999. By then she was newly launched at Fox's Marina at Ipswich and the masts had been stepped. She looked magnificent in the morning sun.

A delegation from the Worshipful Company of Drapers, looked round her that morning and met the newly appointed skipper Dave Bawden. By the time they had left us, they had promised us £25,000 for the vessel's sails.

Dave Bawden and a delivery crew sailed the finished yacht from Ipswich on the east coast to Ardrossan on the west coast via the Caledonian Canal from Inverness to Fort William. They had to contend with gales in the North Sea, but had a quiet voyage from Inverness onwards.

The day before they reached Ardrossan the boat approached the end of the pier at Craighouse on Jura. A fishing boat, very securely tied up to the pier, suddenly fired up its engine at full power as they passed across its stern. The underwater surge from its propeller hit Alba's rudder and spun her round straight into the pier. The boat's bow became wedged between two vertical pillars of the pier.

There was considerable damage to the pulpit rail, and to teak woodwork and fibreglass on each side of the bow. Fortunately, there were no quibbles from our insurers and we got repairs in hand at Ardrossan immediately, as the naming ceremony was only three weeks away. We had to cancel our first two voyages of the season however, with consequent loss of revenue.

The naming ceremony took place beside the Moat House Hotel, Glasgow, on 20 April 1999. Modelled on an RNLI lifeboat naming ceremony, it went very well though the actual naming had to be done in a howling gale and lashing rain. Curly's wife Barbara poured a libation of whisky over *Alba Venturer's* bows, and then we all went into the hotel out of the rain for some musical entertainment and lunch.

I could now look forward to sailing on *Alba* as first mate on the Cutty Sark Tall Ships Cruise in Company from Greenock to Lerwick in the Shetland Islands in August.

Departure after *Alba Venturer's* naming ceremony at Glasgow
(Photograph by Tommy Hutcheson)

Lionel and Barbara Mills *(Photograph by Tommy Hutcheson)*

Chapter 25 – Tall Ships to Lerwick and to Brest

The Tall Ships Races came to Greenock on 30 July 1999, for a four-day stay, attracting 500,000 visitors. The largest sailing event in the world brought fifteen square-riggers and many smaller craft to the port.

One of these was OYT Scotland's *Alba Venturer* and its twelve young crew were sponsored by Rotary Clubs in the West of Scotland. It sailed as the Rotary Boat and flew the Rotary International flag from its crosstrees. Our skipper was Dave Bawden, I was first mate, Mary was second mate, Dave was third mate, and the bosun was Charlie.

I checked in at the boat, and as the crew had yet to arrive, I had a wander round the quays. Greenock was *en fete* on a sunny afternoon. There was a carnival atmosphere around a huge Victorian roundabout and a Ferris Wheel, and the tall ships were impressive. The two largest were the Russian *Kruzenstern* and the Mexican *Cuauhtemoc*. Others included the Norwegian *Statstraad Lehmkhul* and the Polish Naval Academy ship *Oskra*.

In addition to *Alba Venturer*, the Ocean Youth Trust fleet included *Lord Rank* from Northern Ireland, *John Laing* from the south of England, *James Cook* from the north-east of England, and *Greater Manchester Challenge* from the north-west of England.

Our voyage to Lerwick would be a Cruise in Company to

Lerwick in the Shetland Islands, the starting point for a race to Aalborg in Denmark.

The fleet left the Clyde on the afternoon of Monday 2 August. Some vessels were like us bound for Lerwick. Others including the rest of the OYT fleet sailed south to their home ports. Fair winds took us on an overnight passage round the Mull of Kintyre and northwards towards Mull. We anchored at Tobermory alongside the Dutch brigantine *Swan Fan Makkum*.

The next morning was another fine day as we sailed north past the Small Isles of Rum, Eigg and Muck. We saw *Cuauhtemoc* off Eigg, a fine sight with full sail aloft. We anchored overnight at Dun Ban Bay in Knoydart alongside *Swan Fan Makkum*, *Eda Fransen*, *Morning Star of Revelation*, and the famous Falmouth Pilot Boat *Jolie Brise*. A barbecue ashore had to be abandoned when the infamous West Highland midges ate us alive and we retired to our boats to escape them.

The next morning a stiff breeze took us up the Sound of Sleat, through the Kyle of Lochalsh and under the Skye Bridge. A large number of boats anchored alongside us at Tanera Beg in the Summer Isles, and we partied with the crews of the other boats that evening.

We slept well that night, but in the early hours of the next morning we were awakened by a great crash! The wind had changed direction in the night and the OYT ketch *James Cook* had swung on to the shallow rocks at the far end of the anchorage. The tide was falling and she was soon well and truly aground. Her crew were ferried over to *Alba Venturer* where they spent the rest of the night with us.

In the morning the whole of *Cook's* hull was above water. Her skipper and first mate inspected the hull. The steel hull had not been breached, but her rudder was badly damaged. She floated off at high water and was towed into Kinlochbervie by *Alba Venturer* for repairs. Regretfully, her crew had to abandon their cruise but we now continued our passage north.

As we passed Cape Wrath the wind blew strongly from the north-east and to make progress, we had to lower the sails and motor straight into the wind and heavy seas. We met another vessel in the night, which cut across our bows and we were relieved when her navigation lights showed that she had sailed clear of us. We were very tired when we reached Hoswick in the Shetland Islands in the early hours of the morning, where we anchored and were able to get some sleep at last.

We had a day of rest at Hoswick, and a hilarious noisy party in the evening, entertaining each other with games and party pieces.

After breakfast next morning we got the boat ready to enter Lerwick.

In heavy rain we were led by a waiting pilot boat past the 5,000-year-old Broch of Mousa to our berth in the town, which was packed with colourful vessels taking part in the race to Denmark. We were welcomed to Lerwick by the Rotary Club who gave us a reception in a local hotel.

The boat was now cleaned and made ready for the next crew and our crew left for Aberdeen on the overnight ferry. We saw lots of puffins as the ferry passed Fair Isle, whose bird observatory attracts bird watchers from all over the world.

It had been an interesting and eventful voyage through islands and sounds which had been a sea highway for travellers and invaders for centuries.

My next Tall Ships Voyage would take me south to France.

This cruise was an OYT Challenge Voyage on *Alba Venturer* from Troon in Ayrshire, to Brest. From Brest, another crew would take part in a Tall Ships Race to Spain.

The crew were young experienced sailors who were being encouraged to become bosuns and eventually voluntary mates. The Challenge Voyage would be a more adventurous cruise to broaden their experience at sea.

I joined *Alba Venturer* at Troon Marina on Friday 5 July 2002. Our skipper was Trevor Farrar. We briefed the crew that evening about the voyage and reminded them of the deck layout. Most had sailed on *Alba Venturer* before. I checked the crew's passports and found that one belonging to a girl needed to be renewed. There was no way she could get this done in time in Glasgow so we decided to renew it in Belfast.

Our first port of call was Bangor on Belfast Lough. While one of the mates took the girl by train to the passport office in Belfast we carried out some rigging repairs. Two friendly policemen in their new Northern Irish Police uniforms visited us in the afternoon and we watched guillemot chicks in a nest in a crevice in the harbour wall.

We left as soon as our companions returned from Belfast with the renewed passport and made good progress south in fair winds. We had intended to put into the Scilly Isles but the wind continued to favour us so we pressed on to sail through the night to France.

In the morning we approached the Chenal du Four, the sound between the Isle de Ouessant and the Brittany coast. Brest lay just beyond it. Its fast tidal streams and many rocks made it a coast where careful navigation was imperative. I looked for the appropriate charts but could not find them. A hasty recheck by the skipper confirmed my fears that somehow these had been omitted from our chart portfolio, but charts for the onward voyage to Spain were there.

We would have to find a nearby port from which we could get to Brest to buy the charts. Our nautical almanac showed a port at L'Aber Ildut at the mouth of the River Ildut, but looking at the shoreline cliffs we could not see it. We watched some fishing boat sailing past the cliffs, then they suddenly vanished!

We realised the river mouth entrance was concealed. Our almanac had a chartlet of the harbour at L'Aber Ildut and it showed water depths. Checking the current state of the tide, we calculated that there would be sufficient depth for us to enter the harbour.

I now contacted the harbourmaster on VHF radio, speaking in French, and asked for a berth there. He asked us to anchor in the harbour. I asked if he could arrange for a taxi to take me to Brest to buy charts. He agreed to do so. I signed off, and was surprised by a ripple of applause from the crew who had been listening to our conversation.

Half an hour later we were safely in port and I went ashore to meet the harbourmaster. He introduced me to a rather elegant, well-dressed lady who turned out to be my taxi driver. As we drove to Brest she chatted to me about the Tall Ships event in Brest, and was interested to hear about *Alba Venturer*. I bought the charts covering the coast to Brest at a chart agency and returned to the boat by taxi. We were now ready to tackle the Chenal du Four.

The next day we entered the French Naval Harbour at Brest, where all the Tall Ships boats were berthed. It was a very secure area guarded by gendarmes, who rather officiously checked that we were wearing our Tall Ships badges as we left or entered the naval area.

I visited friends on several boats including *James Cook* who had followed us into Brest. Several other OYT boats from England had also joined us. A big feature of Tall Ships events is that the crews of all nationalities mix and visit each other's boats in port.

The French organisers had made a great effort to provide entertainment for the ships' crews, mainly through sporting activities and games. There were traditional Breton Games, archery, radio-controlled boat football, inter-boat football, rowing races, sailing races in Surprise yachts, displays of traditional Breton sailing craft, a Breton bagpipe band, a hurdy-gurdy man, and even a band self-propelled on a cycle made for six!

An evening parade of ships crews marched through the city and were entertained in the city square by local dignitaries.

The time came to go home on 15 July. The crew who were to sail *Alba Venturer* to Spain arrived, and we left by bus for the ferry port of Roscoff. The ferry took us to Plymouth where another bus awaited to take us home.

Over the years I also attended Tall Ships events in Birkenhead and Aberdeen, but the most enjoyable was undoubtedly the event in Brest in 2002.

Alba Venturer off Ailsa Craig *(Photograph by OYT Scotland)*

Early morning watch near Lerwick

Chapter 26 – Dubrovnik

In June 2004 I and three friends decided to charter a sailing yacht out of Dubrovnik in Croatia, and explore the southern group of Dalmatian Islands.

This coast was well known as a superb cruising area and it had spectacular medieval towns all along its length. Many were set up by the Venetians. Dubrovnik itself was founded in the seventh century by Graeco-Roman refugees from the nearby city of Cavtat, which had been sacked by the Slavs. When Slavs also settled in Dubrovnik, the two groups intermingled. This produced a mixture of Latin and Slav cultures unique in the Mediterranean.

Friends who had sailed out of Dubrovnik recommended a Croatian company, Istra Yachting, which we found was actually owned by an American from Delaware. We booked a yacht on-line through its website and paid through a bank account in Austria. I sailed as skipper and George Knight was my first mate. The other crew members were John Ewing and Owen Evans from Barrhead Rotary Club. We had all sailed together before, and got on very well. As George and John were professional engineers and Owen was a C.A. we were well prepared for all eventualities mechanical or financial.

On 19 June we flew by British Airways via Gatwick to Dubrovnik, and a half-hour taxi ride took us to the marina at Komolac, on a river just to the north of Dubrovnik. We checked in at Istra Yachting, I showed my international certificate of competence, and paid a returnable security deposit. The yacht was a brand new Jeanneau Sun Odyssey 37, called *Ragusa*.

We had dinner that night at the Konalic restaurant on the opposite bank of the river, reaching it by a little passenger ferry-boat.

The next morning, we set off down river to the sea, passing under the impressive Tudman Bridge at the mouth of the river, and sailed north in a strong south-east wind. We stopped at the little island of Lapud, where we did some shopping and had lunch, anchored off its fortified monastery. It was a busy place with inter-island ferries calling regularly.

We sailed on in a rising wind to Sipan where we anchored in three metres in a well-sheltered bay surrounded by wooded shores at Sipanska Luka. We would have to anchor here, as is customary, with our anchor holding the bow, and the stern held end-on to the quay by shore-lines. This was going to be difficult as there was a strong cross-wind.

We watched a magnificent large wooden ketch motor in, handled confidently by one man. Motoring into the wind, he dropped his anchor on the run, laid out his anchor chain on the bottom in an s-shaped curve, then turned the boat through 180 degrees and reversed up to the quay, where two waiting men took his two stern lines as he casually tightened up his anchor chain.

It looked so easy, but British yachtsmen find it tricky to back on to a quay as boats do not steer backwards easily. They tend to sheer off to one side or the other. When we attempted this the anchor dragged and we drifted on to a neighbouring Austrian yacht, well protected by many fenders. The skipper shouted at us rudely to go away and was most unhelpful, so we raised the anchor and motored over to a spot close to the main hotel where we re-anchored.

Sipanska Luka had an air of faded grandeur. We had an excellent open-air meal at a restaurant at the old summer residence of some past grandee from Dubrovnik. A kilo of fresh fish and crème caramel went down very well. We returned to the boat in heavy rain and could hear thunder from far off.

On Monday morning a strong south-east breeze took us to the little town of Slano where we bought some provisions. We now set off for the large wooded island of Mljet. At 1230 we were hit by high wind, a rough sea, and a brief thunderstorm with flashes of lightning all around. We saw one lightning strike hitting the sea a mile or so ahead. It soon passed, and half an hour later we arrived at the secluded wooded cove of Okuklje on Mjlet.

We tied up at a berth belonging to the proprietor of the Maestrale Restaurant, who helped us with our lines, as we were not used to the standard mooring technique in Croatia. A permanent heavy 'lazy line' ran along the bottom from a bollard on shore to a buoy moored a couple of boat lengths from the shore. This had to be picked up with a boat hook by a crew member on the bow while the helmsman motored slowly backwards towards the quay. The bow man then secured the lazy line to a bow cleat which halted the boat, and allowed two lines, one from each corner of the transom, to be passed from the stern to be secured ashore. The deal was that you got free mooring if you ate at the restaurant.

Refreshed by an afternoon swim, Owen and I took a walk ashore to a little chapel on the hillside above the restaurant where we ate that evening. On our return to *Ragusa* we found the bay crowded with around forty yachts moored here for the night.

There was little wind next morning as we motored along the coast of Mjjet to the town of Polace, beautifully situated behind small wooded islands at the western end of Mjlet. We tied up at the quay beside a ruined Roman palace right next to a restaurant and a bicycle hirer.

It was a hot sunny afternoon and we hired bikes to visit the verdant Mjlet National Park which had two beautiful inter-connected salt water lakes, Malo Jezera and the larger Veliko Jezera. The lakes catered for all sorts of water sports. We cycled round the wooded shore road of Velica Jezera as far as the Island of St. Mary which had an old Benedictine monastery. It was quite an up and down road back to Palace and as we were all getting on in years, we were quite tired by the time we returned to the boat. It seemed prudent to have a siesta for the rest of the afternoon till it was time to have dinner at the Ogigija Restaurant.

On Wednesday morning it was very hot as we set off at 0930 under engine in a flat calm for the large island of Korcula. At 1020 a light wind let us raise our sails and we had a leisurely sail to the marina at Korcula town next to its ancient fortress.

The medieval walled town was set up by the Venetians and was reputed to be the birthplace of Marco Polo. We wandered around the old town, admired the clock tower and cathedral, and had an excellent meal at Ajio Marie Restaurant.

We began our return journey under engine, again in a flat calm, on Thursday, passing the town of Orebic on the Peljesac Peninsula. We looked into the harbour at Sobra on Mljet, but people ashore stared at us impassively, and did not seem very welcoming, so we continued along the coast to Prozura.

Here we found a beautiful anchorage rather like Caladh Harbour on the Kyles of Bute in Scotland, but larger. The water was very clear with lots of black sea urchins on the rocks. A former fishing village, Prozura, was being redeveloped for tourism and the only fishing now was for its restaurant. We tied up at Marie's Inn's mooring buoy, had an excellent dinner there, and watched the Portugal v. England Euro 2004 football game on TV.

Friday took us back to Dubrovnic, beating all morning into a gentle easterly breeze. On arrival at Dubrovnik we decided to have a look at the city from the seaward side and motored past Bokar Fortress and the towering battlements to look into the busy harbour. We returned to the river mouth, sailed under the Tudman Bridge and filled up with water and diesel at the marina.

At 0900 next morning we handed back the yacht after an underwater check of the hull by a diver. I received my security deposit back intact, and we had a day to spend in Dubrovnik before the flight home.

We could now view the town from the inward side of its walls, and it was an impressive place. During the Croatian Homeland War from November 1991 to May 1992 Dubrovnik was shelled by the Serbs from the heights above the town. Some of the old town roofs were still being repaired. Otherwise, there was no sign of war damage. We looked down at Laza Square, the Rector's Palace and the cathedral, and St. Blaise's statue holding a model of the city.

George and I now walked around the city walls, starting at the Old Port in a clockwise direction. The vantage points on the battlements gave us fascinating glimpses of domestic life in the old city, and its varied red-tiled roofs. From the Bokar Fortress guarding the moat we had impressive views in all directions. We looked down on the Pile Gate, the Franciscan Monastery and Onofrio's large fountain built in 1414. We could see roof repairs on Stradun the city's main thoroughfare, the Jesuit Church, and the Island of Lokrum.

This enjoyable cruise had given us a brief introduction to a beautiful sailing area and we resolved to return in 2005 to explore the islands west of Split further up the coast.

Stradun, the main street in Dubrovnik

Onofrio's Large Fountain, Dubrovik

Chapter 27 – Vis

During the winter of 2004-5 I researched the sailing possibilities of the islands to the south of Split, and made up an itinerary for a fortnight's sailing in May-June 2005 for our second cruise in Croatia. There were many attractive and intriguing places to visit.

On 21 May we flew by Cech Airways from Heathrow to Split via Prague. A half-hour taxi ride took us to the new Kastela Gomilica Marina just to the west of Split, where we joined the boat we had chartered from Istra Yachting. Our yacht was a Bavaria 36 called *Talitha*, named after one of the stars in The Great Bear. In Arabic it means 'the third leap of the gazelle.'

The marina office was closed when we arrived at 2200, but we found the boat on the pontoons. After an anxious search in the dark we found the key to open the boat hatch in a cockpit locker, and were able to settle down for the night. In the morning I paid the security deposit, the boat was officially handed over to us, and we left the marina sailing west in brilliant sunshine and a light wind. Our first stop was at the ancient Venetian town of Trogir founded by the Greeks in the third century BC. We tied up at the ACI Marina, did some shopping, and visited the old cathedral. While we had a delicious steak dinner in a restaurant in the old town a religious procession passed by.

In the morning we sailed to Rogoznica, a village on a beautiful little island connected to the mainland by a causeway.

It had a luxurious American-style marina filled with large expensive motor yachts. Large fishing trawlers were tied up at the village, where we had dinner at Cordoba Fortuna, a very comfortable little restaurant. Our waiter was a Celtic Football Club fan.

When we had tied up, the lazy line had wrapped itself around our propeller shaft. Before turning in I dived under the yacht to free it. The water was agreeably warm.

On Tuesday morning we had a pleasant sail in a moderate northerly breeze to Luka on the island of Prvic, where Croatians took refuge from the Turks in the fifteenth century. We tied up behind the breakwater and had dinner at the Fortuna Restaurant. At 0400 that night we were awakened by the boat bumping into the jetty. The wind had increased and had reversed direction. We pulled the boat off by tightening up our anchor rope and delayed our departure until the high wind had died down at mid-day next day.

We sailed into the large natural harbour at Sibenik on Wednesday morning, and motored up the River Krka and its gorge to Skradin, a holiday haunt of the Romans 2000 years ago. It was the oldest town in Croatia founded in 360 B.C.

We tied up at Skradin, and in the afternoon joined an excursion boat which took us further up the gorge to the Krk National Park waterfalls at Skradinski Buk, a mile or so upriver. This series of falls were quite magnificent. There were seventeen cascades falling over a drop of 500 metres, with lovely pools framed by reeds and trees between each fall. The water poured over white limestone rocks which were being built up by the hard river water, and bathers cooled off in the pool below the last waterfall. Hydroelectric power was generated here at the first D.C. electricity power station built after the station at the Niagara Falls.

On Thursday morning we sailed back downriver to Sibenik, through the narrow entrance to the natural harbour and back towards Split in light winds. We tied up that afternoon at the beautiful island of Primosten.

We had been doing quite a lot of motoring, so I checked the engine oil in the morning and found it was quite low. On the way to Maslinica on the island of Solta, we put into Marina Kremik for an engine oil top-up. As we resumed our journey, we saw a school of dolphins leaping out of the water.

On berthing at the attractive busy port of Maslinica, the lazy line again fouled the prop-shaft and I had to dive under the yacht again to free it. We were berthed beside an eighteenth century fortified villa. Maslinica was a busy place; we watched a fishing boat being hauled ashore, and fishermen mending nets at the quay.

Solta was used in ancient times as a place of banishment for political exiles from Rome, and later as a place of exile for heretics by the Christian Church.

Our main destination for this second week was the island of Vis. During the Second World War it was captured by the British in 1944 and used by Tito as his headquarters for guerrilla activity against the Germans. He was protected at Vis by the Royal Navy and British and American commandos raided Yugoslavia from this island. Scottish soldiers from Vis raided the island of Brac from Vis. The island was quite unspoiled as it had been a military restricted area until 1989.

On Saturday 28 May we motored south for two and a half hours to Vis, and again saw dolphins on the way. It was sunny but the sea was a flat calm with no wind. We reached the town of Vis at 1230, and tied up to the harbour wall opposite a Franciscan Monastery on the site of a Roman theatre. British fortifications beyond the monastery dated from 1811.

As the town was very quiet and it was hot day, we sailed round the western end of Vis to the other town on the island, Komiza. We had to beat against a light west wind, and so it was 1930 before we reached Komiza. Berthing in the harbour with crosswinds was very difficult, but with lots of fenders over the sides to protect the boat next to us we managed to berth at last.

Moments later we had to fend off a huge motor yacht which towered above us and threatened to crush us against the neighbouring boat. We managed to control this monster and once it was safely tied up, its skipper, a very brawny extrovert Croatian apologised for the trouble he had caused and offered us some wine. He passed over six bottles of fine Croatian wine, so we invited him on board to sample our Scottish whisky. It was only as he knocked back a second glass of neat whisky that we realised that he had already been drunk when he had brought his yacht into its berth!

His English was poor but he said he had been a 'hit man' in the Croatian Homeland War and was here to visit his friend, a Croatian general who lived on Vis. He pressed us to come along with him and meet the general, but not wanting to become involved in Croatian politics (some Croatian generals were still on the run for war crimes), we managed to give him the slip as we walked with him along the quay, and passed him into the care of his mortified teenage son who led him back to his boat and bed.

Komiza was a delightful old town with winding narrow alleys. Its waterfront was adorned by palm trees and Venetian style fifteenth and seventeenth century houses with elaborate balconies. Many of those houses were built gable-end on to the sea. The harbour was dominated by the Kastel, a sixteenth century fortress with a slender clock tower.

We celebrated Owen's birthday at a very good restaurant by the sea, Kanoba Bak, for our evening meal, from which we could look across the bay to our boat.

As we left Komiza next morning a very quiet skipper next door appeared on his deck rather sheepishly, and waved us goodbye.

Skradinski Buk, Croatia

The harbour at Komiza, Vis

Chapter 28 – The Inner Dalmatian Islands and Split

We left Vis to explore the islands between Vis and Split, but first we would visit the little island of Bisevo, southwest of Vis, which had a famous Blue Cave. This grotto could only be entered by small boats. It had underwater entrances through which sunlight could enter the cave. The light, reflected off the sandy bottom, filled the cave with blue light.

Our arrival was timed just before noon when light conditions were best for the grotto. We tied up at the pier alongside another yacht. We then got out our little two-man rubber dinghy and outboard, and in two trips chugged round a headland to visit the cave. It proved to be one of the highlights of our cruise.

Outside the cave, a very old little lady in black sat with her dog in a little dinghy tied to a rope stretched across the entrance. She demanded an entrance fee, looking like some character straight out of The Odyssey. We paid up, and she let us paddle into the grotto. A short passage led into the cavern, which was filled with beautiful turquoise light, which illuminated shoals of black fish swimming underneath us. We were lucky to be able to visit the cave, as it is only possible to do so in calm weather.

In the previous year we had visited the eastern end of Korcula and its medieval town. We now decided to visit the port of

Vela Luka at its western end. There was very little wind so we motored for six and a half hours to Vela Luka. Fortunately, the yacht had self-steering gear so we spent the time sunbathing and reading as we made the long crossing.

Vela Luka had a large commercial harbour. We tied up at the quay and went ashore for an evening meal. As we ate our dinner, we could see someone moving our boat further along the quay. We made a hasty return to the yacht and found that the harbourmaster had moved us to make room for a vessel coming in for repair. Rather than spend a night in this busy port we decided to find a quiet anchorage outside the town. As the sun set, we followed a fishing boat out of the harbour and found an ideal spot beside the island of Gubesa in the approaches to Vela Luka, where we slept undisturbed.

We now began the homeward part of our cruise, sailing north towards the large island of Hvaar. We were making for the Pakleni Islands, to the west of Hvaar town and arrived at the little island of Sveti Klement (Saint Clement). We looked for an anchorage near a country restaurant, which had been recommended to us. We found the anchorage in a wooded inlet that afternoon. As we approached in an onshore wind, with one eye on the echo sounder monitoring depth, I chose to anchor between two yachts already anchored there. I decided to sail round the left-hand yacht, motor into the wind till I could drop the anchor, then fall back on the anchor chain until I was between the two yachts and settle there.

It was a manoeuvre I had done many times before and concentration on the task was essential. Imagine my discomfort therefore as I rounded the left-hand yacht to find that four very attractive topless girls were sunbathing with a young man on deck! I felt like Odysseus passing the sirens. Once the boat was secure, we cooled off with a welcome dip amongst shoals of little fishes.

We then lunched in the cockpit trying to ignore the distractions on the other yacht. By now one of the girls was lying nude on the forward deck! Their yacht was flying a German flag, and although it was only a boat's length away, they did not acknowledge us in any way. We hesitated to introduce ourselves in case our motives might be misunderstood. The amused British skipper of the Rival 38 yacht anchored on the other side of us said that he and his wife were still trying to work out the relationship between the young man and the four girls.

Later that afternoon we raised the anchor and sailed in a fresh breeze to the beautifully situated Palmizana Marina on the northeast corner of the island for an overnight stop. We walked back through the woods by a rocky path to the Dionis Restaurant beside our lunch stop, only to find it was fully booked by another party. All we could get was some bread, cheese and wine. After the long walk back to the marina in the fading light we were glad to see its lights gleaming through the trees, and looked forward to a late supper there.

Next morning, we sailed over to Hvaar town where we filled up with diesel fuel and tied up at the busy harbour. Hvaar was a beautiful island whose main crop was lavender. The town was originally a haven for medieval pirates. The Venetians drove them out in 1240 and encouraged the citizens of Stari Grad to move into Hvaar town which became the island's administrative capital.

We visited the cathedral, then climbed the zig-zag path up to the citadel which towers over Hvaar town. It was built by the Venetians in 1550 and strengthened by the Austrians three hundred years later. The views of the off-lying islands from its ramparts were impressive, and there was a constant movement of vessels in and out of the harbour.

In the afternoon we left for Stari Grad on the north coast of the island, passed by the inter-island ferry as we rounded the western end of Hvaar. With a rising wind behind us, we sailed along the north coast and gybed as the wind direction suddenly changed. That meant we let the mainsail boom move over to the other side of the yacht. It is always a tricky manoeuvre especially so in a strong following wind; it makes the boat heel over suddenly. As we gybed there was an almighty crash from down below as the contents of an insecure locker shot out and crashed to the floor. The damage was not too bad, - seven smashed plates. Stari Grad was a quiet little port with fine old quayside buildings, set on both sides of a long narrow inlet. It was founded by Greek settlers from Asia Minor in 385 B.C. We stayed there overnight.

Next day, we sailed to the town of Bol on the large island of Brac. As we approached Bol we passed the only sandy beach in the area, with swimmers enjoying themselves in the sun. It was a sand spit called Zlatni Rat, deposited there by coastal currents. Bol was another very busy little port with attractive old buildings. Over the centuries it had been harried by Saracens, Turks, and almost any other force passing by.

We sailed westward until we came to the gap between the islands of Brac and Solta. We put into the lovely town of Milna on Brac and tied up at the marina alongside a boatyard working on wooden boats. During the Napoleonic Wars Milna was for some time a Russian protectorate.

On Thursday 2 June we sailed over to Split on the mainland, and tied up at the marina at the west end of the city. We walked along the seafront past some interesting and colourful old houses. We explored the old part of the town and we could see pieces of the Roman Emperor Diocletian's palace built into old buildings, - Roman arches, pillars, forums, and even two Egyptian sphinxes dating from fifteen B.C. The palace was surveyed in 1757 by the Scottish architect, Robert Adams and his finds influenced his future work in Britain.

The cathedral was very prominent, with a gleaming white exterior and a very dark interior. At its heart was Diocletian's mausoleum. When the cathedral was built his remains were replaced by the remains of Christian martyrs whom he had executed.

A day had been kept in hand to allow for possible delays due to bad weather, and so our last day was spent sailing off the island of Ciovo with a lunch stop at Sveti Fumija near Trogir. We returned to Kastela Marina where we filled up with diesel fuel and spent our last night on board. The next morning, the yacht was inspected, our security deposit was returned, and we handed the boat back to the charter company. In the afternoon we flew back to London. We had achieved a lot on this more extensive cruise, sailing 287 nautical miles in all, in marvellous sunny weather, to fascinating places. Our destination in Croatia in 2006 would be the Kornati Islands near Zadar.

Talitha at Hvaar

The quay at Hvaar

Chapter 29 – The Kornati Islands and Zadar

We returned to Croatia for our third cruise on 20 May 2006, flying from London to Split. A long taxi ride then took us to Sukosan, just south of the city of Zadar. We collected our yacht here in the evening from Adriatic Charter at the Marina Dalmacia. Again we chartered a Bavaria 36, called *Polaris*.

In the morning we set off in a moderate south-west breeze for Bozava at the north end of the long island of Dugi Otok. We sailed through the passage between the islands of Uglijan and Otok Rivanj, past the southern end of Otok Sestrunj and across to Bozava. We tied up at the breakwater just before the arrival of the inter-island ferry.

From Bozava our route next day took us north through rocky islands passing between Skarda and Ist. As we approached the gap, George remarked that according to our GPS satellite navigation system we were now a hundred metres ashore on an islet to our port side!

A close look at the chart revealed a small note saying that for our chart and satellite positions to coincide we had to add a correction of a quarter of a nautical mile of east longitude to the satellite longitude. This put us back safely into the sea. The reason for this was that the chart datum and satellite datum did not quite coincide. This did not matter very much well offshore, but inshore near rocks and small islands, we trusted our eyes more than the GPS.

We sailed on in a light south-east wind to the beautiful wooded island of Silba, with a lunch stop at the island of Ist, and reached Silba at 1645. That night we enjoyed excellent steaks at Konoba Mul restaurant.

Silba was once famous for its sailing fleet, which transported goods from Venice to Dalmatia. The era of steamships led to its decline.

Next day, we sailed in a light south-west wind to Suzak which we reached at mid-day. However, we did not linger there as a gale warning persuaded us to sail on to the more sheltered port of Malo Losinj. John spotted a turtle in the water as we left Suzak. The gale arrived in the night and as there were still high winds next morning, we spent Wednesday 24 May exploring this part of the island of Losinj.

At 0800, we watched a yacht pass through the channel which cuts through the long island at its narrowest part. It motored straight into the heavy seas battering the north coast of Losinj. A swing road bridge opened twice a day to let boats pass through. We walked along the quayside toward the town centre set around the head of the inlet. Mali Losinj had a big fishing fleet and we watched fishermen handling huge nets for catching tuna.

The town was attractive with a second marina and colourful buildings all around the narrow bay. We heard that the neighbouring village of Veli Losinj was worth a visit so took a local bus to it over the hill, and found a lovely little fishing harbour with attractive cafes around the water's edge. Owen and I returned to Mali Losinj by a three-mile path along the shore.

Our route now took us south between Losinj and Ilovik, then on to the island of Ist with a lunch stop at Premuda. Ist was a sleepy little fishing village and we found a berth beside the local ferryboat.

In the morning we motor-sailed in very light winds through a string of islands to Veli Iz on Otok Iz. Veli Iz was a busy port, with a large water tanker moored at the quay which serviced the arid Kornati Islands. There were many yachts moored here, as it was a popular jumping-off point for these islands.

The Kornati Islands were uninhabited and could only be visited by excursion boats or yachts. Anchoring or mooring was restricted to designated places. The islands were barren but dramatic. Many were cone shaped and the limestone strata were very contorted.

We entered the archipelago on Saturday 27 May through Proversa Mala, a very narrow channel between the islands of Dugi Otok and Otok Katina. There were dramatic cliffs on the western side of Dugi Otok where we found a sheltered spot for lunch at Lucina Bay.

In the afternoon we sailed to Telascica Bay, a sheltered wooded inlet at the southern end of Dugi Otok, the 'long island', and anchored at Mavrovica at its head where the Duke and Duchess of Windsor had spent part of their honeymoon. We were visited by a National Park warden and charged fifty kuna each for entry to the area.

On Sunday morning we sailed south past the red and white lighthouse on Veli Silo and found ourselves in the middle of an early morning yacht race. Navigating the narrow channels was tricky.

We passed the sixth century Byzantine Fortress of Tureta on the island of Kornat, and the little medieval Church of Our Lady of Tarak. Beating into a moderate south-east breeze, down the western coast of Piskera we passed through a narrow channel into the large Marina Piskera tucked away on the small island of Otok Vela Panitula. Owen and I climbed the little hill above the marina to photograph the magnificent vistas all around.

On Monday morning we left the marina by its northern entrance and in a high following wind we sailed on a run, over to the Murter peninsula on the mainland.

By the time we approached the marina at Jezera on Murter, the wind had risen considerably and had built up a following sea with high waves. To reach the marina we would have to move the mainsail boom over to starboard. Rather than do this by gybing, which could be dangerous in the high wind, we decided to do what the old square-riggers did, which was to 'wear ship'. We put the engine on to get more power, then swung the boat round through the wind on to the other tack to move the boom over safely. We eased the mainsheet, and continued our fast run to Jezera.

It was a struggle in the strong cross-wind to moor the yacht at the marina pontoon, but we finally managed it. The next boat had even greater difficulties and got entangled with moored boats. The harbour launch had to pull her clear.

The strong wind continued next day but was now from the south-west, ideal for our sail north-west to the Kornati island of Zut. As we reached the southern tip of Zut we saw a small yellow flying-boat. We anchored for a lunch stop at Pinizelic Bay but made a hasty departure when the anchor dragged. We reached Zut at 1430 and tied up at its marina at the northern end of the island. Heavy rain fell after our arrival.

The next day was hot and sunny and the water was completely

still as we motored north behind a catamaran. Visibility was excellent and the mainland mountains were clear and dramatic. Altogether it was a beautiful morning.

Its peace was suddenly shattered as a low flying, double-piston-engined, yellow amphibious aircraft roared across our bows and landed in the water just ahead of us. It taxied for a short while then rose up and flew towards a hillside where it jettisoned its cargo of water. It was obviously a fire-fighting plane, which could scoop up water from the sea. It turned, then made another pass, this time landing on the sea behind us. The plane exercised all morning as we continued our journey north.

As the temperature rose, inverted mirages of mainland buildings appeared on the horizon. At 1230 we stopped for lunch at Mala Rava on the island of Otok Rava. In the afternoon a gentle north-west breeze allowed us to put up our sails and run south to the road bridge between Uglijan and Pasman. We passed under it and tied up at Kuklikje harbour on Uglijan.

On Thursday 1 June we started off for Privlaka on the coast to the north of Zadar in a moderate easterly wind. However, at 1330 a very strong north-east wind obliged us to reef down, and we decided to make for Zadar instead. At 1515 we arrived at Zadar Marina and tied up in a large commercial harbour.

Zadar was the ancient capital of Dalmatia, was held by the Venetians for centuries, and was Italian-speaking for many years. It was ceded to Italy in 1921, and became part of Tito's Yugoslavia in 1947. It was now a major port in the Adriatic.

Our yacht lay just opposite the old town, and we crossed over by a little passenger ferry sculled with a single oar in the stern by a dexterous ferryman. We visited the ninth century

Church of St. Donat, and the cathedral whose belfry was built in 1898 by an English architect T.G. Jackson.

We heard strange musical sounds that night and next morning we crossed over again by another little ferryboat to see Zadar's sea organ. Its sounds came from large grilles in a series of steps leading down to the sea and were produced by waves pushing air through thirty-five underwater organ pipes.

On Friday 2 June we returned the yacht to Marina Dalmatia at Sukosan, after filling up with diesel fuel. We had sailed 284 miles on the cruise and had run up twenty-six and a half engine hours.

We travelled back to Split Airport by coastal bus, but our BA plane to London had a one and a half hour delay, due to a technical fault. We would have missed our connection to Glasgow had our pilot not been scheduled to fly our next BA plane to Glasgow.

Our three cruises to Dalmatia had been enjoyable and eventful. There were traces of man's activities here for centuries. It had been a wonderful coast to explore, with many places still unspoiled, beautiful and remote.

Harbour ferry, Zadar

Old Town of Zadar

Chapter 30 – Journey's end

The three Croatian cruises marked the end of my odyssey. I had now been sailing yachts for twenty-nine years including twenty-one as an Ocean Youth Trust mate. By June 2006 I had logged 17,205 nautical miles. When I reached my seventies, I no longer had the muscular strength of my earlier years and the pain of osteo-arthritis had begun to affect my knees. I had to give up my daily morning jog, and replace it with swimming three times a week to keep fit.

In 2012 and 2013 I had both knees replaced. The operations were successful but my mobility was now restricted. My support for sailing became shore-based.

I remained a member of Ocean Youth Trust Scotland, which had helped me to develop my sailing skills, and had given me the confidence to sail beyond my native shores. I owe it so much, and I am delighted that it is now recognised as one of the U.K.'s leading sail-training organisations. Now in its twenty-first year of operation, I wish Ocean Youth Trust Scotland and its patrons Lionel and Barbara Mills every success in the future.

During my busy teaching career, I valued my sailing as it let me relax in a parallel and totally different environment. I enjoyed sharing experiences afloat with my sailing companions, and I enjoyed the refreshing company of the many young people who sailed with me in my watches.

Sailing *Rum Runner* had also given me much pleasure. I had

enjoyed the frisson of excitement as she speeded up in a rising wind, and the satisfaction of pilotage to remote anchorages. I learned a lot carrying out maintenance work when she was ashore, and it was always exciting to see her launched for each new sailing season.

My cruise in Australia was a life-enhancing experience, and I loved every minute of *Alba Venturer*'s building, launching and successful cruising.

The West Coast of Scotland was an ideal place for me to develop my seamanship, and to enjoy its wonderful seascapes and wild life. I have many happy memories of sailing.

Acknowledgements

Some of the material in this book first appeared in articles I wrote for Yachting Life in the 1960s, which published many accounts of Ocean Youth Club activities.

I am grateful for photographs provided by Ocean Youth Trust Scotland, and Ocean Youth Trust South. I am also indebted to Tommy Hutcheson, former Ocean Youth Trust Northern Ireland Area Governor, for photographs taken at *Alba Venturer*'s naming ceremony. The photograph of my slalom canoe was taken by the former commercial photographers, Star Photos of Perth, and I thank Ross Ritchie for his photograph of *Rum Runner* in the Kyles of Bute.

Lastly, I have appreciated the encouragement, guidance and support I have received from my publisher and editor James Essinger of The Conrad Press, his book designer colleague Charlotte Mouncey, and the efficient typing services of Margaret Dowley.